Globalisation

Paul Streeten

Globalisation

Threat or Opportunity?

Copenhagen Business School Press
HANDELSHØJSKOLENS FORLAG

Globalisation – Threat or Opportunity?

© *Copenhagen Business School Press*, 2001
Cover designed by Kontrapunkt, Denmark
Printed by Laursen Grafisk, Tønder
Printed in Denmark
1. Edition. 2. Impression 2001

ISBN 87-630-0084-9

Distribution:

Scandinavia
DJØF Publishing/DBK, Siljangade 2-8, P.O. Box 1731
DK-2300 Copenhagen S, Denmark
phone: +45 3269 7788, fax: +45 3269 7789

North America
Copenhagen Business School Press
Books International Inc.
P.O. Box 605
Herndon, VA 20172-0605, USA
phone: +1 703 661 1500, fax: +1 703 661 1501

Rest of the World
Marston Book Services, P.O. Box 269
Abingdon, Oxfordshire, OX14 4YN, UK
phone: +44 (0) 1235 465500, fax: +44 (0) 1235 465555
E-mail Direct Customers: direct.order@marston.co.uk
E-mail Booksellers: trade.order@marston.co.uk

Table of contents

1. Introduction

Born, though only just, into the expiring Austro-Hungarian Empire, having spent most of my life in post-imperial Britain, having come to post-Watergate, post-Vietnam America in 1976, I regard myself as something of an expert in imperial decay. Having moved from Austria to England, Scotland, and America, my roots are not in the soil, but are aerial, across national boundaries. These facts have turned out to be useful for examining the post-hegemonic world. The USA still claims to be the world's leading (though not imperial) power, but compared with the period before 1970, there is some evidence of the diminished giant syndrome, at least comparatively.

When I joined Boston University in 1980 a small group of faculty members got together and reflected on what would be the next intellectual breakthrough. This is, of course, a nonsense question. For if we knew what the next intellectual breakthrough would be, we would already have made it and it would be the latest breakthrough, not the next. In any case, we decided that it would be "globalisation" and arranged a regular seminar on it. This was before the days when globalisation had become a buzzword on everybody's lips and to be seen in (almost) every newspaper, periodical and book.

As Daniel Bell has said, the state has become too small for the big things and too big for the small things. Too big for the small things means that we should delegate to lower levels of decision-making - local authorities, non-governmental organisations, the civil society - issues that are better dealt with by them rather than by central government. Decentralisation has joined liberalisation, deregulation and privatisation as the imperatives of our age. This is not the question with which this book is concerned. But the need for certain issues to be delegated upwards, to international, transnational or global processes and institutions, is.

The book begins with a rapid review of the past, a brief survey of the present, and a glimpse at the future. I identify four functions of any international system concerned with development and discuss how they were, are, and will be exercised. Coordination of the four functions promises gains for everyone. Globalisation is transforming trade, finance, employment, migration, technology, communications, the environment, social systems, ways of living, cultures, and patterns of governance. The spread of universal ethical norms is to be welcomed, just as the encouragement and nurture of the diversity of local cultures should be celebrated.

The growth of technology and globalisation mutually reinforce each other. Much of the process of globalisation is historically not unprecedented, but the information and knowledge technology (as well as materials technology, biotechnology and laser technology), the setting, the absence of a single dominant centre, and certain features such as the replacement of trade in raw materials by manufactured products and of inter-industry by largely intra-industry trade are new. International interdependence is growing, and to some extent and partially, so is international integration. But it is accompanied by disintegration and fragmentation of other parts of society. Partial global economic international integration (mainly of the élites), without global policies and institution, leads to national social disintegration.

The frequently adopted notion that globalisation is the same as international integration (or global interdependence) is not tenable. There are at least six reasons for why partial international integration leads to national disintegration:

1. "Downsizing," "restructuring," "delayering," and "reengineering" (words that are not part of my active vocabulary) have reduced the demand for low-skilled workers in the rich and middle-income countries and kept the wages of those who succeeded in keeping their jobs low.
2. Stemming the brain drain in developing countries makes egalitarian incomes policies impossible. To prevent too many of the professional and skilled people from leaving they have to be paid something not too far out of line with their pay in the rich countries.
3. Tax revenues to pay for social services have been reduced as a result of globalisation, though the need for them has increased.
4. The élites in the low-income countries are opting out of national commitments and take as their reference group the élites in the advanced countries. This leads to the neglect of essential social services like education and health in their own countries. Members of the élites in the low-income countries have their medical and

surgical treatment in the advanced capital cities of the North. They send their children to the schools in the North. They take their vacations there, do their shopping there, and visit relatives who have settled there. They invest their money on the stock exchanges of the rich countries. As a result, they have no interest in improving the medical, educational and economic facilities in their own countries. Local "capacity building" is not part of their agenda.

5. The culture of the élites is global and estranged from the culture of the local people.
6. The tendency for minorities to break away from their country and form independent nations, resulting in the proliferation of states, can be explained by their desire to participate directly in the benefits of globalisation.

Is globalisation a threat to humanity or groups within it or is it an opportunity? A tentative balance sheet is drawn up. Markets, to be efficient, have to be embedded in a framework that enables their productive potential to flourish and to be used for socially and ecologically sustainable development. The reduced power of national governments combined with the spread of world-wide free markets and technological innovation without a corresponding authority to regulate them and hold them accountable has contributed to the marginalisation of large regions and groups of people. The state has become to some extent ungovernable, while the global society is ungoverned. While some groups acquire unprecedented wealth, unemployment, poverty, inequality and alienation are increasing, partly (though not solely) as a result of this process. Crimes, drugs, terrorism, violence, civil wars, diseases, and environmental destruction are also becoming globalised. In the struggle of international competition capital, technology and high skills dominate the more readily dispensable factors unskilled labour and the environment. Competition forces firms to reduce costs, and labour and nature suffer.

Among the actors on the global scene are governments (central, provincial and local), regional organisations, multinational corporations, national and international voluntary associations, and the United Nations and its agencies. Different authors want to allocate different roles to these agents. The implications of these trends for the international movement of ideas, technologies, firms (small and large, national and multinational, public and private), money, and people are analysed.

The book begins with a discussion of the notions of integration and interdependence between nations. It then deals briefly with the main aspects of globalisation, namely trade, global financial flows, technology and transnational corporations, and international convergence of real wages. Next, the concern is with the beneficial and harmful aspects of globalisation. I examine the impact of globalisation on growth, productivity, unemployment, income distribution, technology and institutions, as well as on culture. I then discuss the role of government in the era of globalisation. One generally expects the scope of government to be diminished as globalisation proceeds. Instead, I argue that globalisation and free markets call for not less government but for more, as well as pressures from below, from the civil society. A section is devoted to the informal sector in which many of the growing number of poor people work. I argue for institutional arrangements that use the strength of the large firms for the benefit of the small ones. This is the judo trick.

The case for human adjustment loans to developing countries and the impact of international cooperation on people are next examined. I show that adjustments to free trade and globalisation are costly and may not always be wholly desirable. The improvement of existing and the creation of new global institutions are discussed and arguments are advanced against excessive preoccupation with what is feasible and in favour of utopian thinking. There follow sections on social capital and globalisation, international migration, comparisons between East Asia and Africa, the case for and against regional arrangements, and the positive role of conflict in international relations. Finally, I outline the implications of globalisation for analysis and research, and for international action and policies.

2. Integration and interdependence[1]

We read everywhere that international *integration* is proceeding rapidly as the result of the increased flow of trade, capital, money, direct investment, technology, people, information and ideas across national boundaries. International integration implies the adoption of policies by separate countries as if they were a single political unit. The degree of integration is often tested by whether interest rates or share prices or the prices of goods are the same in different national markets. Integration, however, can be a term loaded with positive value connotations. Although there may be some objections to the unwanted imposition of uniformity, and although the disintegration of a pernicious system may be desirable, it would generally be regarded as improper to advocate "disintegration." But it is possible for integration to be defined either with or without such value premises. The value premise can be that all members of the integrated area should be treated as equals, either with respect to certain opportunities, such as access to the law, jobs, trade, credit, capital and migration, or with respect to certain achievements, such as a minimum standard of life, education and health services. In this sense of integration equalising common taxation and social services are implied. If we omit this particular value premise and confine integration to mean equal economic opportunities, however unequal the initial endowments of members of the integrated area, the world was more integrated at the end of the nineteenth century than it is today.[2] Although tariff barriers in countries other than the United Kingdom were higher then (20 to 40 per cent compared with 5 per cent in 1990), non-tariff barriers were much lower; capital and money movements were freer under the gold standard (i.e. without the deterrent to trade of variable exchange rates); and movement of people

[1] I am grateful to Ajit Bhalla, Al Berry, Louis Emmerij, Hans Singer and especially to Ronald Dore, for helpful comments on earlier drafts.

[2] It is the non-historical touting of the current trend to globalisation that has led critics to call it globaloney.

was much freer; passports were rarely needed and citizenship was granted easily. Today, international migration is strictly controlled. Between 1881 and 1890 the average annual rate of immigration into the USA was 9.2 per 1000, reaching over 10 in the first decade of this century. Between 1991 and 1997 the average annual rate of immigration was 3.8 per 1000 of US population.[3]

If we include the value premise of equal treatment, the world is, of course, even less integrated. International inequalities are today greater than ever before. Dani Rodrik uses the term "international economic integration" instead of "globalisation."[4] He does this for two reasons. "First, while not as trendy, my term has a distinct meaning that will be self-evident to economists. Globalization, by contrast, is a term that is used in different ways by different analysts. Second, the term "international economic integration" does not come with the same value judgements – positive or negative – that the term "globalization seems to trigger in knee-jerk fashion."[5] It will be seen that I disagree with both reasons. "Integration" is ambiguous and comes also with or without value judgements. Rodrik illustrates the unparalleled prosperity and integration of today's economy by a chart showing rapid growth of exports. But this, of course, does not show anything of the kind.

The four functions that are coordinated in an integrated international system that aims at development are today fragmented.[6] These are (1) the generation of current account surpluses by the centre; (2) the financial institutions that convert these surpluses into loans or investments; (3) the production and sale of producer goods and up-to-date technology; and (4) the military power to keep peace and enforce contracts. Before 1914 they were exercised by the dominant power, Great Britain; between the wars there was no international order, Britain no longer being able and the USA not yet willing to accept the functions; for quarter of a century after the last War they were exercised and coordinated by the USA. But today we live in a schizophrenic, fragmented world, without coordination. The surpluses were generated in the 70s by a few oil-rich Gulf sheikdoms, later by Germany and Japan, and today mainly by Japan. The financial

---

[3] U.S. Census Bureau: Statistical Abstract of the United States (1999) p. 2.

[4] Dani Rodrik (2000) pp. 177-178.

[5] Rodrick (2000) pp. 177-178.

[6] See Paul Streeten (1989).

institutions have mushroomed all over the world; not only in London and New York, but also in Tokyo, Hong Kong, Singapore, Frankfurt, Amsterdam, Zurich, the Cayman Islands, The Isle of Jersey, the British Virgin Islands, Cyprus, Antigua, Liechtenstein, Panama, the Netherlands Antilles, the Bahamas, Bahrein, Luxembourg, Switzerland, etc. And the economically strong countries such as Germany and Japan were strong partly because they did not spend much money on the military.

Non-tariff barriers for trade imposed by the OECD countries and restrictions on international migration have prevented fuller global integration. The result is deflation, unemployment, and slow or negative growth in many countries of the South. But the present fragmentation provides us for the first time with the opportunity to coordinate these four functions and to build a world order on equality, not dominance and dependence. It is a challenge to our institutional imagination to design ways of implementing this new order.

It may be objected that there is no reason why different countries or agents, without coordination should not exercise the four functions. But the historical evidence and theoretical considerations show that coordination is necessary if we are to avoid inflation and unemployment in the North, stagnation and underemployment in the South, and growing inequality and slow growth in the world as a whole. The global public goods of world prosperity, stability, growth and peace cannot be provided by uncoordinated laissez-faire. Without coordination the current account surpluses will be invested in the USA and Europe instead of in the capital-hungry South, the financial institutions will be media of speculation instead of productive investment, and the industries, including the potential export industries in the North, will be partly underemployed.

Between 1870 and 1914 the world was integrated unwittingly. By imposing fewer objectives on government policy (such as those mentioned in the next paragraph), and by accepting what later, in retrospect, appeared to be irrational constraints, such as the gold standard, and consequentially fixed exchange rates, and lack of freedom to pursue expansionist monetary policies, and the constraint of balanced budgets, different countries were integrated into a single world economy. It was dominated by one power, Great Britain. Domestic policies were severely constrained by the need to adhere to the gold standard. Today the constraints on national policies consist in the activities of multinational companies and banks. Before 1914 the world had been more integrated than it is today. International integration, however, was no guarantee of peace. It did not prevent the First World War.

Later, many objectives of government policy were added to the nightwatchman state's duty to maintain law and order: among them full employment, economic growth, price stability, wage maintenance, reduced inequality in income distribution, regional balance, protection of the natural environment, greater opportunities for women and minorities, etc. The rejection of constraints on policy such as fixed exchange rates, and limits on the discretion of monetary and fiscal policies, led to greater integration of national economies by permitting policies for full employment and the welfare state; but at the same time they led to international disintegration. Such disintegration is, however, entirely consistent with a high degree of international *interdependence*. For interdependence exists when one country, by unilateral action can inflict harm on other countries. Competitive protectionism, devaluation, deflation, or pollution of the air and sea beyond national boundaries are instances. A nuclear war would be the ultimate form of interdependence resulting from international disintegration. Today global market forces can lead to conflict between states, which contributes to international disintegration and weakened governance.

Interdependence is measured by the costs of severing the relationship. The higher the costs to one country, the greater is the degree of *dependence* of that country. If a small country benefits more from the international division of labour than a large country, its dependence is greater. If high costs from severing economic links were to be incurred by both partners to a transaction, there would be *interdependence*.

It is quite possible to have intensive and rapidly growing international *relations*, without a high degree of interdependence. This would be so if the relations could be abandoned at low costs. There could, for example, be a large and rapidly growing trade in slightly different models of motor cars, produced at similar costs, but there would be not much deprivation or loss if buyers had to substitute home-produced models for imported ones. The index of interdependence would be the consumers' and producers' surpluses, not the volume, value or rate of growth of international trade.

There is a different sense of "interdependence" according to which "dependence" means only "influenced by," without great benefits from maintaining, or costs from severing, the relationship. In this attenuated sense there can be interdependence even though the costs of cutting off relations are low or even negative. But this is not a useful sense for our purposes.

International interdependence is often said to be strong and to have increased. International trade is taken to be an indicator of interdependence and its high and, with some interruptions, rapidly growing values are accepted as evidence. Between 1820 and 1992 world population increased five-fold, income per head eight-fold, world income 40-fold, and world trade 540-fold.[7] Sometimes international financial flows are taken as the measure of interdependence. But five important qualifications to the notion that globalisation is unprecedented, large and increasing are necessary.[8]

First, if we consider the ratio of international trade to national income, the rapid growth of the postwar decades can be taken to be a return to pre-1914 values after the interruptions of two world wars, the Great Depression, and high levels of protection.[9] The share of world exports in world GDP rose from 6 per cent in 1950 to 16 per cent in 1992. For the industrial countries, the proportion increased from 12 per cent in 1973 to 17 per cent in 1992. For 16 major industrial countries the share of exports in GDP rose from 18.2 per cent in 1900 to 21.2 per cent in 1913.[10] This was largely the result of dramatic reductions in transport costs, as well as of the decline in trade barriers such as tariffs and import quotas and of the opening of new markets such as China and Mexico. The comparisons in the ratios are very similar for particular countries.[11]

The total ratios of trade to GDP are, however, misleading. Over the post-war decades the share of services, including government services, in GDP increased enormously. Many of these are, or were until recently, not tradable. If we were to take the ratio of international trade to the production of goods only, it would show a substantial

[7] Angus Maddison (1995).

[8] See Paul Streeten (1989) pp. 1153-186. For a more recent sceptical treatment of the claim of globalisation, see Robert Wade (1996).

[9] It is often said that globalisation is irreversible. But the history of the two wars and the inter-war period shows that it is highly reversible. After having reached a peak in the late 19th century, it retreated until after the second World War.

[10] Deepak Nayyar (1995) pp. 3-4; A. Maizels (1963) A. Maddison (1989) P. Bairoch (1993).

[11] This increase in the trade/GDP ratios occurred in spite of a general increase in tariff protection between 1870 and 1913. It was therefore not the result of trade liberalisation. In the pre-1913 period of globalisation the role of the state increased, not declined. See Paul Bairoch and Richard Kozul-Wright, Globalization Myths (undated).

increase not only compared with the inter-war period, but also compared with the time before 1913.

The second qualification to the notion that unprecedented globalisation is now taking place is that the developing countries, and the groups within these countries that have participated in the benefits from the growing trade (and also from foreign investment, which is highly concentrated on East Asia, Brazil, Mexico and now China) have been few, not more than a dozen, and no poor ones among them. Twelve countries in Asia and Latin America accounted for 75 per cent of total capital flows, while 140 of the 166 developing countries accounted for less than 5 per cent of inflows.[12] A large share of foreign investment is made by firms from a handful of countries, in a narrow range of industries.[13] The large, poor masses of the Indian subcontinent and of Sub-Saharan Africa have (at least so far) not participated substantially in the benefits from the growth of international trade and investment. In fact, the bulk of the international flow of goods, services, direct investment and finance is between North America, Europe and Japan. The group of least developed countries accounted for only 0.1 per cent of total global investment inflows and for 0.7 per cent of inflows to all developing countries. Africa in particular has been almost completely bypassed.[14] More than 80 per cent of world population living in developing countries account for less than 20 per cent of world income.[15]

The third qualification is that direct foreign investment constitutes a smaller portion of total investment in most countries than before 1914. Domestic savings and domestic investment are more closely correlated than they were then, implying that even investment capital is not very mobile. This is explained partly by the fact that government savings play a greater role today than they did in the past, and partly by floating exchange rates that raise uncertainties and are a barrier to long-term commitments. The same point is made by noting that, though gross capital flows are very large, net flows are not. Current account deficits and surpluses are now a much smaller proportion of countries' GDP than they were between 1870 and 1913. Britain ran a current account surplus that averaged 8 per cent of GNP

---

[12] Alejandro López-Mejía (1999).

[13] World Investment Report (1996).

[14] TEP The Technology/Economy Programme *Technology and the Economy; The Key Relationships* (1992) p. 233.

[15] See UNDP (2000).

and invested this overseas, compared with 2-4 per cent for the West German and Japanese surpluses (and the American deficit) in the 1980s. But the fact remains that this is surprising in view of the talk of the globalisation of capital markets. The bulk of foreign investment has been the capital import of the USA and the outflow from Japan.

Foreign capital, mostly loans, financed one third of domestic investment in New Zealand and Canada in the late 19th century, and one quarter in Sweden. Today it accounts for ten per cent in a few developing countries. Today's foreign investment is more broadly based than it was in the 19th century, is more short-term, more speculative and less stable. 19th century globalisation produced greater stability than today's.

The fourth qualification is, as we have seen, that there is much less international migration than in the earlier period. Barriers to immigration are higher now than they were then. As we have seen, passports were unnecessary and people could move freely from one country to another, to visit or work. 60 million Europeans moved to the Americas or to Australia or other areas of new settlement. In 1900 14 per cent of the American population was foreign born, compared with 8 per cent today.[16]

The fifth qualification is the already mentioned fact that it is not the volume or value or rate of growth of trade that should be accepted as an indicator of economic interdependence, but the damage that would be done by its elimination, i.e. consumers' and producers' surpluses. These are difficult to measure. But we know that much trade is conducted in only slightly differentiated goods, which could readily be replaced by similar domestic products without great loss to buyers or great increases in costs.

On the other hand, a small and slowly growing volume of trade could be of great importance and lead to substantial losses if it were cut off. Like a link in a bicycle chain, it could, though small, make a big difference to the working of the whole system. The United States, for example, depends strongly on quite small imports of manganese,

---

[16] On the other hand, electronic technology has made labour mobility much less important than it once was.

tin and chromium. Before World War I trade was largely conducted in the form of an exchange between raw materials and manufactured products, for which consumers' and producers' surpluses are large. Today the bulk of trade is intra-industry and even intra-firm trade of often similar manufactured products for which these surpluses are much smaller. Indeed, manufactured goods contain parts from so many countries that it is not possible to attribute their origin to any one country.

The process of globalisation, according to some definitions, means opening-up to trade or liberalisation. In the last decade such liberalisation was followed mainly by the ex-socialist countries, which turned away from central planning in order to link up with the world economy, and by the developing countries, which changed from import-substituting industrialisation to export-orientation accompanied by a partial dismantling of the state. This move was not the result of entirely free choices, but was itself a response partly to global forces, partly to pressures by the World Bank, the International Monetary Fund in their stabilisation and structural adjustment programmes, and the words and doctrines of state minimalism of the rich countries, and partly to the hopes of benefiting from global gains.

Some OECD countries, on the other hand, have put up additional non-tariff barriers such as so-called voluntary export restraints, procedural protection most notably in the form of anti-dumping actions, and specific subsidies to exports of goods and services competing with imports. The Multifibre Arrangement and the Common Agricultural Policy of the European Union are blatantly protectionist devices. Other barriers have been raised against steel, electronics and footwear.

Trade is, of course, only one, and not the most important, among many manifestations of economic interdependence. Others comprise the flow of factors of production, capital, technology, enterprise and various types of labour, across frontiers; there is also the exchange of assets, the acquisition of legal rights, of information and knowledge. The global flow of foreign exchange has reached the incredible figure of $ 2 trillion per day, 98 per cent of which is speculative. The multinational corporation has become an important agent of technological innovation and technology transfer. In 1995 the sales of multinationals amounted to $ 7 trillion. Their sales outside their home countries are growing 20-30 per cent faster than exports.

As Jeffrey Williamson has shown, another aspect of globalisation is the convergence of real wages in different countries.[17] Since the 1950s the gap between American and European wages has shrunk markedly. Similarly, in the second half of the 19th century European wages caught up with American ones. In Europe, some countries closed the gap with Britain, then the Continent's leader. In a later paper Jeffrey Williamson argues that economic integration (rather than, say, better education in the low-wage countries) was the main cause of this narrowing.[18] As a result of the growth of international trade the prices of traded goods became more alike in different countries. The relative prices of the abundant factors of production in each country rose (land in America, labour in Europe), while those of the relatively scarce factors fell (labour in America, land in Europe). A recent study confirms this.[19] Emigration from Europe to America also helps to explain the rise in wages in Europe and their containment in America.

After about 1895 the losers from international integration began to revolt and the claims for protection and restrictions on immigration became louder. Between the two wars the international order broke down. Today's low-skilled workers in America and other advanced countries may similarly claim that the economic rise in the South is a threat to them. The voices of Ross Perot and Patrick Buchanan in America and Sir James Goldsmith and Jean-Marie Le Pen in Europe gave shape to these alarms. In the developing countries corresponding visions are calling for a reversal of the trend towards globalisation. But, in spite of rising unemployment, the political forces of nationalism are losing out against the economic forces of globalisation.

In addition to economic interdependence (trade, finance, direct investment) there are educational, technological, ideological, cultural, as well as ecological, environmental, legal, military, strategic and political impulses that are rapidly propagated throughout the world. Money and goods, images and people, sports and religions, guns and drugs, diseases and pollution now move quickly across national frontiers. When the global satellite communications system was established instantaneous communication from any part of the world to

---

[17] Jeffrey Williamson (1995) The comparisons of real wages are in terms of purchasing power equivalents.
[18] Jeffrey Williamson (1996).
[19] Kevin O'Rourke, Alan Taylor and Jeffrey Williamson (1996).

any other became possible. It is not only the creation of a 24-hour money market that had become possible, but also the flashing of pictures of statesmen and film stars across the globe, making these faces more familiar than those of our next-door neighbours.[20]

We hear much of the creation of a borderless world and the end of the nation state. It is true that satellites and the Internet have greatly increased the speed at which the communication of cultural and informational impulses is propagated throughout the globe. Americans fly British airways, drive Japanese cars and drink Russian vodka. A German firm, Daimler-Benz, buys a quintessentially American company, Chrysler Corporation and Michael Gorbachev does Pizza Hut commercials.

But here again, as in trade and investment, vast areas in the poor South are either left out (subsistence farmers are not affected by global forces), or suffer the backwash effects of globalisation, and the rise of particularism and religious fundamentalism is a sign that many people protest against it. In Russia, support for Gennady Zyuganov, head of Russia's resurgent Communist Party, shows the backlash against globalisation.

It has become a cliché to say that international interdependence is great, has increased, and will continue to grow. Normally this is intended to refer to trade, foreign investment, the flow of money and capital, and the migration of people. Advances in technology such as the jet, telex, satellite TV, container ships, super tankers, super ore carriers and technical progress in transport, travel and, above all, in communication and information have shrunk the world. By reducing the cost of communication, technology has helped to globalise production and finance. Globalisation, in turn, has stimulated technological progress by intensifying competition, and competition has forced the introduction of new technology. Globalisation has spread its results widely through foreign direct investment. History may not have ended, but geography, if not coming to an end, certainly matters less. And the interaction of technology and globalisation has presented new problems.

The international spread of ideological and cultural impulses is at least as important as that of economic impulses. Observe the young

---

[20] Anthony Giddens (1995). As Mark Blaug has pointed out, there has been no similar globalisation in economic theory. "Almost all Italian economists know everything there is to know about Sraffa and yet one can travel far and wide in the United States without ever meeting an economist that has even heard of Sraffa. Such is the insularity of academia!" Mark Blaug (1998) p. 1926.

in the capitals of the world: from Ladakh to Lisbon, from Maine to Mozambique, from West Virginia to East Jerusalem, from China to Peru, in the East, West, North, and South, styles in dress, jeans, hair-dos, T-shirts, jogging, eating habits, musical tunes, attitudes to homosexuality, divorce, abortion, have become global. Even crimes such as those relating to drugs, the abuse and rape of women, embezzlement and corruption have become similar everywhere. But although American cultural influences are important, there are many other influences and no single dominant power.

"The super-rich are seceding from their nations. So what you have is not a Western or East Asian or Southeast Asian or Chinese model. We are building enclaves of super-privilege. What you're having is not a global village but a series of global ghettoes. The Western élite is not the sole villain," said Palagummi Sainath, the author of *Everybody Loves a Good Drought*, a critique of government and the establishment in India, based on his reporting from some of the poorest villages in the country.[21] Partial international integration, once again, leads to national disintegration.

"There is a new catchword in the developing world...to cover cultural wounds not believed to be strictly Western, Eastern or self-inflicted; the word is globalization. It wraps up all the fears of somehow losing control to foreigners, felt as much by Americans who hate the United Nations and immigrants as it is by Indians or Filipinos who feel threatened by the International Monetary Fund, Kentucky Fried Chicken, Joe Camel or Time Warner. That shrinking world everyone was so proud of a decade or so ago has become a cultural strangler."[22]

But the impression of global uniformity can be deceptive. Just as trade, foreign investment and the flow of money have affected only a few regions of the world and left the rest comparatively untouched (except for some negative effects), so this globalisation of culture is only partial. It is evident in the towns and suburbs, and the more advanced countryside. The poor in the rural hinterlands, in spite of the spread of transistors and television, have been largely bypassed. And in many lands there has been a reaction to tradition and tribalism. Global integration has provoked national disintegration. Globalisation has posed a threat to the rootedness on which community life depends.

---

[21] Quoted by Barbara Crossette (1997).

[22] Barbara Crossette (1997) p. 5.

Ethnic or cultural passions are fracturing societies and regions. We witness Islamic fundamentalism in the Muslim world. Evangelical fundamentalism is spreading not only in the USA, but also in East Asia, Africa, and Latin America, often linked to a Calvinistic, entrepreneurial ethics of saving and hard work. Hindu fundamentalism is evident in India and has led to the most horrific bloodletting (though Hinduism cannot, strictly speaking, be fundamentalist because it is a religion without dogma) and Judaic one in Israel. A recent decision of the Knesset, yielding to he pressure of a minority of fundamentalist rabbis, denies the right of Conservative and Reform rabbis to perform valid conversions for those wishing to become Jewish.

Nations have broken up into smaller, ethnic groups. All this is partly a reaction against westernisation, the alienating effects of large-scale, modern technology and the unequal distribution of the benefits from industrialisation. In the ex-Soviet countries the assertion of ethnic identities is the result of the weakening powers of the state in the face of globalisation. The complaint is that development has meant the loss of identity, sense of community and personal meaning. The Taliban in Afghanistan deny women jobs, force them to dress in a subservient manner and prohibit girls going to school. Algeria's Islamic Army of Salvation, the military arm of the banned Islamic Salvation Front, according to Amnesty International "executed" 100,000 people since early 1992 when the authorities cancelled a general election in which the radical Islamic party had taken a lead. People in many countries assert their indigenous cultural values. This assertion of indigenous values is often the only thing that poor people can assert. Traditional values bring identity, continuity and meaning to their lives. Between the two opposite forces, globalisation on the one hand, and the assertion of peoples' identities on the other, between what Benjamin Barber calls Jihad and McWorld,[23] states have found their base undermined.

But the same trend, the proliferation of states, can also be explained by an opposite tendency. The increase in the number of countries in the last ten years can be explained, paradoxically, as a result of globalisation. In a world united by air travel, the Internet, multinational enterprises and international organisations, ethnic minorities wish to participate directly in the benefits promised by globalisation. These people of the new states feel that their old

---

[23] Benjamin Barber (1995).

countries had denied them the opportunities to participate in the affairs of the world. But the rise in the violent expression of ethnic tensions cannot be so easily explained. Rwanda, Burundi, Bosnia, Armenia, Azerbaijan, Chechnya, Kosovo, the Kurds, the Palestinians, the Chiapians have manifested degrees of violence after having lived with their neighbours sometimes for generations in peace. Violence has often been the result of the breakdown of a previous order. Democratic elections in countries without the tradition and institutions of democracy such as courts, police, a free press, often led people to have recourse to ethnic violence.

Technology, communications and market forces are unifying the world, while at the same time ethnic, religious and racial tensions are breaking up the world into small tribal fragments. According to Benjamin Barber, Jihad and McWorld are diametrically opposed yet intertwined forces. "Jihad not only revolts against but abets McWorld, while McWorld not only imperils but recreates and reinforces Jihad."

What Barber calls "retribalization" is a violent process where "culture is pitted against culture, people against people, tribe against tribe, a Jihad in the name of hundred narrowly conceived faiths against every kind of interdependence, every kind of artificial social cooperation and mutuality: against technology, pop culture and integrated markets."

Globalisation makes national government more difficult. Monetary and fiscal policies run up against the impact of global tides as people, international banks and multinational corporations avoid the intended results by sending or spending their money abroad or attracting money from abroad. The obligations of extended families, government and religion disappear as people leave their rural communities to live in large cities. Recently enriched members of the middle class with links to politicians and officials often use their newly acquired powers in corrupt ways that counteract traditional values.

The difficult task is to build modernity on tradition. Japan has succeeded in this. Traditional consumption habits and community loyalties have contributed, until recently, to the fantastic economic growth of the country. Neither all tradition nor all modernity is to be welcomed. The repressive nature of both some traditional values and structures and some modern ones is evident. Tradition can spell stagnation, oppression, inertia, privilege; modernisation can amount to alienation and a loss of identity and sense of community. Traditional cultural practices such female genital mutilation, sexual subjugation, attacks on and killing of women with too small dowries, kerosene burning and honour killing, widow burning (sati), child marriage, female infanticide, domestic battering, wife beating, prevention of women's education, female ritual slavery, cannibalism, slavery, exploitative and hazardous child labor, debt bondage, witchcraft, demon worship, ritual sacrifice, punishment of criminals by amputation, and other barbaric habits are objectionable and should not be tolerated. There is no moral case for abstaining from stopping these native customs, however traditional.

All this suggests that the perception is of a greater degree of globalisation and integration than has in fact occurred. Foreign investment is a smaller proportion of GNP than it was before 1914. Transnational corporations are more domesticated than some of the literature suggests. Most of them hold most of their assets and have most of their employees in their home country and conduct the bulk of their R&D there. This is confirmed by the fact that in the second half of the 1980s 89 per cent of US patents taken out by 600 of the world's largest firms listed the inventor as a resident of the home base.[24] Hence strategic decisions and innovations come from the home country. This may, however, be replaced by a wider global spread of R&D as a result of telematics, the convergence of computer, communication and control technology.

The movement of people is severely restricted, much more than it was in the nineteenth century. Although it is true that states are more constrained than they used to be, from above by global economic forces and from below by peoples (minorities, tribes, ethnic groups) asking for rights, participation or independence, reports on "Sovereignty at Bay" (Raymond Vernon) "The Twilight of Sovereignty" (Walter Wriston), "the End of the Nation State" and "Borderless World" (Kenichi Ohmae and others) are therefore somewhat premature. The illusion of rapidly increasing globalisation arises from a short time perspective that looks only at the last 30 or 40 years, at the beginning of which countries were exceptionally closed as a result of the Great Depression and World War II.

Views on the benefits and costs of the global mobility of the different items, such as trade, finance, technology and ideas, differ. In a much-quoted passage Keynes wrote "Ideas, knowledge, art, hospitality, travel - these are things which should of their nature be international.

---

[24] Robert Wade (1996)

But let goods be homespun whenever it is reasonably and conveniently possible; and, above all, let finance be primarily national."[25] Today it is more fashionable to deplore the "cultural imperialism" or the "homogenisation" of television and the mass media and the global spread of mass culture, and to attempt to confine culture to local knowledge, activities and products, while advocating free trade in goods and services.

Neoliberals advocate free trade and a good deal of laissez-faire but not the free movement of people. François Quesnay had added to laissez-faire laissez-passer, but this is forgotten today, perhaps because contemporary liberals fear that it would accelerate population growth (or reduce the pressures to reduce it) in the low-income countries of emigration and therefore not contribute to raising their welfare, or that it would interfere with economic objectives (especially the level and distribution of income), or cultural values, or social stability and cohesion, or security, in the country receiving the migrants. But all these objections also apply to the free movement of goods and services. In any case, there is an inconsistency.

Globalisation can be considered according to its impact on various objectives. We shall analyse its impact on: (1) growth and productivity; (2) employment and skills; (3) wages and inequality (both within and between countries) of income and wealth; (4) technological and institutional innovations; (5) cultural autonomy and diversity; (6) human security; (7) military security and peace.

---

[25] J. M. Keynes (1933) p. 237. As Dani Rodrik points out, the rest of the paragraph is not quoted as often: "Yet, at the same time, those who seek to disembarrass a country from its entanglements should be slow and wary. It should not be a matter of tearing up roots but of slowly training a plant to grow a different direction." Dani Rodrik (1997).

3. Uneven benefits and costs of globalisation

Globalisation has helped to create undreamed of opportunities for some people, groups and countries. Human indicators such as literacy, school enrolment, infant mortality, and life expectancy have enormously improved in the last few decades. In low- and middle-income countries life expectancy has increased from 46 years in 1960 to 64.4 years in 1998; infant mortality per 1,000 live births has fallen in the same period from 149 to 64; adult literacy rates have risen from 46 to 73 per cent; and real GDP per head from $ 950 to $ 1,250.[26] The Cold War has ended and the prospects of peaceful settlements of old disputes have improved from West Asia to South Africa and Northern Ireland. Democracy has spread throughout the world and replaced autocratic regimes. Between 1986 and 1996 the portion of the world's states with democratically elected governments jumped from 42% to 61%. Globalisation has been particularly good for Asia, for the global growth of production, for profits and for the owners of capital and sophisticated skills. (See Table.)

At the same time, the economic restructuring, liberalisation, technological changes and fierce competition, both in the markets for goods and for labour, that went with globalisation have contributed to increased impoverishment, inequalities, work insecurity, weakening of institutions and social support systems, and erosion of established identities and values. Liberalisation and reduced protection of agriculture, by reducing agricultural supplies, have raised the price of food (compared with what it would otherwise have been), and food importing countries have suffered as a result. Globalisation has been bad for Africa, and in many parts of the world for employment (see below the section on unemployment), for those without assets or with rigidly fixed and unadaptable skills. International competition for

---

[26] UNDP (2000).

markets and jobs has forced governments to reduce taxation and with it social services that had protected the poor,[27] and cut public services and regulations that had protected the environment, has forced governments and firms to "downsize," "restructure" and "re-engineer" and has made necessary all kinds of steps to ensure that the cost of labour is low.[28]

Between 1972 and 1986, for developing countries as a whole, social expenditure as a proportion of total government expenditure declined from 35 per cent to 27 per cent and for industrial market economies from 58 per cent to 56 per cent (World Bank 1988). Between 1980 and 1993, in the Philippines health expenditure declined from 4.5 per cent to 3.0 per cent, and in Kenya from 7.8 per cent to 5.4 per cent. (World Bank 1995). In Latin America, despite recovery of social expenditure in 1991, expenditure per head on health and education was lower than in 1980-81. (IDB, 1996, p. 47).

At the height of the welfare state, in the quarter century after World War II, when it was thought that a government can steer the economy to full employment and keep it there, national integration had been accompanied by international disintegration. Though people had expected full employment to remove the case for trade restrictions, there were at least four (not equally good) reasons for trade restrictions and for limiting access of imports of labour-intensive products in conditions of full employment. The first and most obvious reason is the fact that full employment policies (and even more so over-full employment policies) make for stronger inflationary pressures and therefore tend to aggravate balance of payments problems if the country's inflation is greater than the average rate in its trading partners. Balance of payments difficulties resulting from inflation are perhaps not good reasons, but they are often used as excuses for trade and foreign exchange restrictions.

The second reason is that full employment policies were often interpreted (or perhaps misinterpreted) as policies that guarantee particular workers their present jobs. Transitional unemployment was not easily distinguished by its victims and their representatives from lapses from full employment. While it would be clearly a mistake to

---

[27] But see the section on government and open economies in which a positive relation between the size of government and public expenditure ratios is suggested. This could be the result of pressures to compensate those adversely affected by globalisation.

[28] It should, however, be remembered that downsizing in companies such as AT&T, Nynex, Sears, Philip Morris and Delta Airlines cannot be attributed to international competition. Businessmen like to blame global forces for actions for which they should bear responsibility.

identify full employment in a growing and changing society with a prescriptive right to existing jobs in particular occupations and regions, it should be remembered that change and transition have social costs. The better off a society is, the more it can afford to forgo extra increases in income and production for the sake of less disruption, particularly if such disruption continues to be called for repeatedly or if its benefits are mainly enjoyed by others than its victims. (See section 22 on "the case for a quieter life.") If full employment policies were interpreted in this way, they would present a new motive against admitting more imports.

The third reason is that according to the Stolper-Samuelson theorem labour-intensive imports tend to reduce the absolute incomes of unskilled and semi-skilled workers. This is so because the relative price of the product intensive in this type of labour will fall after trade liberalisation. Unless there is a perfect system of compensation, it is understandable that these groups resist the removal of trade restrictions.

The fourth reason is that in conditions of full employment the terms of trade argument for protection, also called the optimum tariff argument, comes into its own. If resources are unemployed, the nation can export more and simultaneously raise everybody's income. But in conditions of full employment national gains may be at the expense of other nations. In particular, it becomes important to keep the prices of imported necessities as low as possible. It is not to be expected that many governments have imposed tariffs in order to improve their terms of trade. In any case, trade restrictions imposed for other reasons must often have led to higher barriers than those indicated by the optimum tariff argument. Nevertheless, there may be conditions in which the restrictions are not above the optimum and then governments are for good reasons reluctant to remove them because this would lead to a deterioration in the terms of trade below the optimum. To wish to avoid a loss is rather different from trying to snatch a gain at the expense of others.

It is for these and similar reasons that in the quarter century after World War II national integration led to international disintegration, in spite of what is regarded in retrospect as a golden age. Now the situation is reversed. After the early 1970s (partial) international integration has led to national disintegration. (See also section 5, the impact on income distribution.) Beveridge and Keynes had to be dismissed in the face of the pressures of globalisation, which weakened the pursuit of national monetary, fiscal and social policies, while at the same time weakening organised labour.

The Zapatista guerrillas held a convention in 1996 in the jungles of Southern Mexico entitled "The Intercontinental Forum in Favour of

Balance sheet of globalisation
(Rough approximations)

Good for:	Bad for:
Japan, Europe, North America East and South East Asia (until 1997)	Many developing countries Africa (exceptions: Mauritius and Botswana) and Latin America (exceptions: Chile and Costa Rica)
Output	Employment
People with assets	People without assets
Profits	Wages
People with high skills	People with few skills
The educated	The uneducated
Professional, managerial & technical people	Workers
Flexible adjusters	Rigid adjusters
Creditors	Debtors
Those independent of public services	Those dependent on public services
Large firms	Small firms
Men	Women, children
The strong	The weak
Risk takers	Human security
Global markets	Local communities
Sellers of tech. sophisticated products	Sellers of primary and manufactured products
Global culture	Local cultures
Global peace	Local troubles (Russia, Mexico, Turkey)
Advocates: businessmen, economists	Environmentalists, working people, consumer rights groups, family organisations, farmers, religious organisations, advocates of democracy, Zapatistas

Humanity and Against Neo-Liberalism." The closing session met in a steamy, mudhole amphitheatre and ended with the Zapatistas doing a kind of drum roll and denouncing the most evil, dangerous institution in the world today. To a standing ovation, the Zapatistas declared the biggest enemy of humanity to be the World Trade Organization in Geneva, which promotes global free trade.[29]

But it is not primarily critics from the Left who have pointed to the excesses and threats of globalisation, but the capitalists themselves. The 1997 meeting of the World Economic Forum in Davos - the assembly of the world's free-market elite - was devoted to ways of ameliorating the worst consequences of global competitiveness. George Soros, the multibillionaire financier, wrote an article for *The Atlantic Monthly* entitled "The Capitalist Threat." In Europe, the chief executives of some of the largest companies are voicing doubts about the European Monetary Union.

As Table 1 and Table 2 show, the share of the developing countries in the global distribution of wealth has shrunk between 1960 and 1994. Even in the rich countries unemployment, homelessness, crime, and drug abuse have grown. New conflicts have replaced old ones, terrorism is widespread, and people's lives have become more insecure. New technologies, new types of organisation, low-cost competing imports, and immigrants have made redundant large numbers of semi-skilled workers.

In the poor countries poverty, malnutrition, and disease have grown side by side with improvements in living conditions. Nearly one third of the population in developing countries and more than a half of Africa's live in absolute poverty. In 1992 six million children under five years died of pneumonia or diarrhoea. 23 million people are classified as refugees. The dissolution of the old system of the extended family, together with the increasing reliance on market forces and the dismantling of state institutions, has left many victims of the competitive struggle stranded and helpless.

Globalisation and the economic progress that goes with it have proceeded unevenly in time and in space. The rise in income per head has differed widely between countries and regions, so that income gaps have widened. Income disparities between the rich and the poor nations have doubled over the last thirty years.

---

[29] Thomas L. Friedman (1997).

Whereas at the end of the nineteenth century the main agents on the international scene were states, dominated by Britain until 1913, and by the United States for a quarter of a century after World War II, today transnational corporations and international banks have joined states and to some extent replaced them. The world's 37,000 parent transnational corporations and their 200,000 affiliates control 75 per cent of world trade. One third of this trade is intra-firm.[30] The principle guiding their action is profit. At the same time, very few of these firms are genuinely transnational or even international (Shell and Unilever are the exceptions in being at least genuinely duo-national, British and Dutch). Most other companies that operate in many countries are stamped by the country of their headquarters. As we have seen, the prediction that sovereignty would be at bay and that the nation state, confronted with ever larger and more powerful transnational corporations, would wither away, was, like reports of Mark Twain's death, somewhat exaggerated. Many countries have successfully dealt with, regulated and taxed these firms.

The new technology, combined with deregulation and privatisation, has contributed to the uneven impact of globalisation. The new and rapidly growing information technology depends on institutions, infrastructure, skills and policies, which generate oases of activity and growth in the midst of desert zones.

In addition to states and private companies and banks, there has been a growth of international non-governmental, non-profit organisations and voluntary agencies that form the international civil society. There are also the multilateral institutions such as the United Nations and its agencies, the World Bank, the International Monetary Fund, the regional development banks. The beneficiaries from the activities of the non-governmental organisations and the multilateral institutions have often been not the poorest but the better off among the small entrepreneurs. There has been polarization even within the informal sector. Some enterprises have done very well and graduated into the formal sector, while others have barely survived. Finally, there are the international labour unions, which are weak compared with national unions. Globalisation that relies solely on market forces further weakens the power of both national and international labour unions.

---

[30] UNRISD (1995), p. 27.

It does not follow that developing countries would have been better off had they closed themselves off from the process of globalisation and tried to become autarkic. Joan Robinson said that there is only one thing that is worse than being exploited by capitalists, and that is not being exploited by them. The same goes for participation in globalisation. Those with skills and assets take advantage of the opening up to globalisation, those without them get left behind. But there are better options than to allow these people to become the victims of the blind forces of globalisation. Measures such as social safety nets, guaranteed employment schemes and training provisions to cushion poor people in low-income countries against being battered by these forces, should be built into the system of international relations. This is necessary not only for political stability, but for reasons of our common humanity.

4. Unemployment

Globalisation has led to the need of firms to compete internationally, and international competition has reinforced globalisation. Cost reductions, greater efficiency and higher incomes have been achieved at the expense of growing uncertainty, unemployment and inequality.

Globalisation has reduced the ability of national governments both to maintain full employment and to look after the victims of the competitive struggle. Unemployment is an evil the costs of which far exceed incomes or output lost. It destroys self-respect, breaks up marriages, encourages crime and can lead to suicide.

Persistent high unemployment in most OECD countries has been a leading policy issue in the last two decades. At first, it was thought that the oil price rises in the 1970s and the deflationary policies pursued in response to them were the cause of the deterioration in employment. But as these high unemployment levels persisted into the 90s and as oil prices and other commodity prices fell since 1986, the explanation had to give place to others. Overvaluation of some exchange rates has contributed to high unemployment. Some of the high unemployment has been attributed to globalisation and to the new technologies of information and communication. The impetus to some of the new technologies has been globalisation and the international pressure of competition, and the new technologies have promoted globalisation.

Kurt Vonnegut, in his novel *Player Piano*, describes a future nightmare society in which the divine right of machines, efficiency and organisation has triumphed, and the large underclass of unemployed are handed out, by a small group of affluent managers, plenty of goodies, but lack what John Rawls regards as "perhaps the most important primary good," which is self-respect. Vonnegut's unemployed eventually revolt.[31]

The concern in the advanced countries has become jobless growth. In fact economic growth, whether measured in terms of overall productivity or productivity in manufacturing, has been considerably slower since 1981 than in the sixties, when growth was not accompanied by unemployment. Since the growth of productivity has been less than the growth of demand, one would have expected jobs to be created rather than destroyed.[32]

There was a slowing down of productivity growth and a growth of unemployment. The growth of output of goods and services without more unpleasant work, with more agreeable leisure is, of course, to be welcomed, not condemned. It is what we mean when we say that productivity per worker has increased. While some authors today regard employment as a basic need, Sidney Webb, the co-founder of the Fabian Society and the London School of Economics, more properly regarded leisure as a basic need. Many forms of monotonous, dirty, hard or dangerous work are a burden, not a blessing. The foundation for the salvation of humanity lies in the growth of productivity. Increases in output per worker are to be welcomed. But this is only so as long as either of two conditions is met. Either demand and output must grow rapidly enough to absorb all those seeking work. There is no reason in theory why this should not be so. Although the new technology displaces workers, it also lowers costs and therefore either lowers prices or raises money wages or profits. In each case the demand for goods and services, and therefore for labour, is increased, though it will take time to retrain and relocate the labour.

Alternatively, the productivity gain can be taken out in the form of leisure or other forms of satisfying activity (or passivity). The reduced work load can then be spread evenly, with corresponding equally distributed rises in incomes. Various imaginative proposals have been made about flexible worktime, sabbaticals for workers, allocating time to high-tech self-provisioning, to freeing time for doing

---

[31] Ronald Dore reminded me that what deprived the underclass of self-respect was the fact that it was an "equality of opportunity" society. IQ tests decided who became a manager and it took a manager to lead the revolt. Were you to allocate jobs by a lottery or the accident of birth, there would be no problem with self-respect.

[32] See John Eatwell (1995) p. 273.

things one really wants to do, etc.[33] The main point is that the time- and labour-saving effects of the new technologies should be widely spread, and not be maldistributed between an over-worked group of workers and the unwanted unemployed.[34]

These two conditions, or at least the first, were met in the Keynesian golden age after World War II. But if, as has been the case in the OECD countries in the last decade, output grows insufficiently fast to generate employment for the whole workforce, and if the workload is unevenly distributed, part of the workforce working hard and long hours while the rest is unemployed, we find ourselves in a society in which John Kenneth Galbraith's private affluence amid public squalor is joined by private affluence amid private squalor. Anyone walking through the streets of New York or London has witnessed the homeless sleeping in mid-winter in the open. Whether the cause of growing unemployment is the globalisation of economic relations, inadequate growth of demand (due to government policy resulting from fears of inflation and balance of payments crises), technological change that calls for new skills that are and perhaps will remain scarce, weaker trade unions, deregulation, immigrant workers or low-cost imports from developing countries, the unemployed underclass does not even benefit from Vonnegut's handouts. They lack both recognition and necessities. Doing "more with less" (as a popular classic on re-engineering puts it) is good for economic growth and for the economy, while people become superfluous. The market does not nurture the dignity of those who lose their jobs or live under the threat of losing them. A recent headline in the *Wall Street Journal* ran: "No Need to Fear Lower Unemployment."[35]

Jobless growth is not confined to the advanced countries. China has been enjoying spectacularly high growth rates, but unemployment, particularly urban unemployment, has become a major problem.[36] The result of globalisation and foreign competition (in goods and labour

---

[33] Limiting hours worked by the government is, however, not a solution. Only if weekly pay is reduced might shortening working hours lead to higher employment. Even then, recruitment, training and other fixed costs may make it less profitable for a firm to employ more workers for shorter hours. If it becomes more difficult to coordinate a larger workforce, productivity will fall. For these reasons decreeing shorter working hours is not the solution; permitting greater flexibility may contribute to one.

[34] In his essay *Economics for our Grandchildren* (1929) J. M. Keynes predicts that we shall all be working only 5 hours a week by the year 2000.

[35] James Annable (1996) who is chief economist at the First Chicago Bank.

[36] See A. R. Khan (1996).

markets) has been the need to cut unit labour costs. Previously the state and collective firms had practised a concealed system of unemployment insurance, a kind of indoor unemployment relief. All members of the labour force had been guaranteed employment, which meant gross over-manning of factories. When China began to be integrated into the global economy it had to reduce labour costs and attract direct foreign investment. In 1986 a new regulation decreed that employment in state enterprises had to be based on fixed-term contracts for three to five years, and enterprises were granted the power to dismiss workers. In 1988 a State Bankruptcy Law was introduced that made it possible to liquidate or restructure state enterprises with resulting reductions in employment. The decline in employment was sharpest in collective enterprises, 15.5 per cent between 1991 and 1994. Without unemployment insurance and alternative ways of earning a living, the unemployed have contributed to an increase not only in China's inequality but also in growing poverty in the midst of spectacular, unprecedented high growth rates. However, China's high economic growth rate promises to absorb most members of the workforce.

Similar growth in unemployment has occurred in many ex-socialist countries. Though official unemployment figures for Russia are low, there has been substantial withdrawal from the labour force and non-registration of many of those thrown out of employment.

The desirability of free consumers' choice between different products has been rightly emphasized. But most people spend more time and have more at stake working and producing than consuming and buying. Free producers' choices are therefore at least as important as free consumers' choices: the ability to choose between jobs and activities should be given at least the same weight as the ability to choose between different brands of detergents or different models of cars or different television channels. But general unemployment, combined with an inadequate number of vacancies, deprives workers of this choice, as well as of the means (earnings) with which to exercise consumers' choice. Security of employment is also important as the means of access to food security, satisfaction of basic needs, access to health and education, and the other objectives of human development. In order to enable people to exercise their free choices as producers a situation of over-full employment is necessary. There must be more vacancies than job-seekers, so that there can be free choice of jobs. Of course, full employment and over-full employment imply that the choices of the employers are reduced. This accounts for their opposition. But employers are fewer than workers and normally are better off. It also spells higher inflationary pressures or open inflation, which accounts for the opposition of some electorates. Some claim that inflation hits the poor more than the rich and is worse for them than unemployment. And full employment is sometimes misinterpreted as the right to remain employed in any given job, which can be a recipe for stagnation.

Among the basic human needs are not only food, water, health, sanitation, shelter, transport, education, and protection from harm and injury, but also job security. Job security is as important as food security, both in itself and as a means for securing food security. If job security is to be achieved in a progressive economy, it cannot mean tenure in given jobs, for these will change with technical progress, changing demand, and trade liberalisation, but the option, if dismissed from one job, to enter a new job.[37]

The current justification for the existence and tolerance of widespread unemployment and for not raising the general level of effective demand is different in industrial, ex-socialist, and developing countries. In industrial countries it is the fear of inflation and of balance of payments difficulties that prevents the achievement of full employment. And inflation may hit hard the same groups of people who are hit by unemployment. The difficult and as yet largely unsolved task is to design a strategy that combines (1) full or over-full employment with (2) absence of inflation, and (3) free wage bargaining and democratic government. This happy triangle has so far been found to be elusive. It seems that a reserve army of unemployed or a less metaphorical army of police and soldiers has so far been the only options for avoiding inflation.[38]

The efficiency wage literature has pointed out several reasons why the quality of labour and the efforts of those who are employed are improved as a result of the existence of unemployment. This justification of unemployment is quite distinct from and additional to

---

[37] Ron Dore has pointed out that job security can mean security in the same employment if the company is Japanese and transforms itself through diversification and adaptation to the changing structure.

[38] Hans Singer has pointed out that the Golden Age of the Keynesian consensus of the 1950s and 1960s proved that this happy triangle is in fact possible if the necessary mild controls of inflationary pressures are accepted. The critics would reply that it took two decades for the workers to see through the money illusion.

that of avoiding inflation. Higher than equilibrium real wages combined with unemployment are justified in this literature on the ground that they improve both the ability and the willingness of workers to work harder and more effectively. An important forerunner of these writers, Karl Marx, already wrote of the need for a reserve army of unemployed to make capitalism work. The recent literature has put new clothes on Marx's analysis and discusses it in terms of the principal and agent relationship, and the inability to monitor properly the effort every worker puts into his work. Unless workers then fear unemployment, they will slacken and reduce their efforts. The higher than market-clearing wages have the function of disciplining the workers.

Quite apart from the reduced opportunity to exercise free choice, unemployment also reduces the incentive for those with jobs to accept new, labour-saving innovations, if they are liable to lose their jobs as a result. This effect seems to have been ignored by the efficiency wage literature. On the other hand, as the evidence from Eastern Europe shows, over-full employment can have detrimental effects on product quality and variety, product and process innovation, and workers' and managers' discipline.

Another approach, that of the insider-outsider model, comes to similar conclusions. A small, mainly male, insider élite workforce coexists with poorly paid, not fully recognised outsiders. One group of workers - the insiders - are not perfect substitutes for others, who may be unemployed - the outsiders. They have more experience, are better motivated and more committed to the firm. Together with the capital and management of the firm they generate a rent, for part of which they bargain. Their higher wages, and their resistance to hiring the outsiders, keep the outsiders out. Such polarization has occurred in the USA, at least until the second half of the 1980s. After that there has been a shift towards advocating reduction of the insiders and expansion of the outsiders in the service of "flexibility." Europe, by contrast, has shown throughout the post-war history greater job security, high wages and high social benefits, combined with a more rapid growth in unemployment.

A third approach, suggested by Robert Solow,[39] is to analyse the labour market as a social institution, and to attach the notion of fairness to a higher wage than that which would equate total demand for and

---

[39] Robert M. Solow (1990).

supply of labour. The unemployed then do not underbid this wage, in their self-interest, because at some later date they expect to benefit from it. Were they to offer themselves at lower wages now, all workers would be thereafter worse off. Although it would be in the interest of anyone worker to underbid, whether others do the same or not, this would lead to a Prisoner's Dilemma outcome, everyone being worse off than had they refrained from underbidding. Repeated "games," however, lead to adherence to the norm that prevents such mutually destructive and ultimately self-destructive outcomes.

The answer to the employment problems created by globalisation lies in the right combination or package of government policies. Simple Keynesian remedies, such as expanding effective demand, appear not to work any longer, though the experience of 1996-1999 in the USA suggests that much so-called structural unemployment disappears if labour markets are tight.[40] Even low-skilled workers have found jobs when demand was sufficiently high. But, nevertheless, many unemployed are long-term unemployed. Expansion of demand would rapidly produce an excess demand for labour, since employers would reject the long-term unemployed as unsuitable. Once a person has been unemployed for more than a year, he becomes very unattractive to employers. There would then be a rise in money wages and prices without a reduction in unemployment. Imports would grow (and jobs would be created abroad) without the ability to match them by exports. Among the measures additional to expanding demand are usually education and training programmes for workers, both to achieve higher productivity and to reduce unemployment without inflation, income support for low-paid workers, wage subsidies to employers, tax policies that create jobs and prevent environmental degradation, population controls, and social safety nets.

On the other hand, there are those who say there is no need to fear inflation, that inflation is dead. Global competition and corporate restructuring will keep prices down while productivity gains will let growth flourish.

What about those whose disabilities in the light of globalisation, the information and communication revolution, and rapid technological change - lack of learning ability or self-confidence or self-discipline - render them unemployed and perhaps unemployable? This raises the

---

[40] Before the second World War much of unemployment had been diagnosed as structural. But with the very high level of demand caused by the War, this unemployment completely disappeared.

set of problems that used to be discussed under the heading of structural unemployment, or later, mainly in Latin America, marginalization, or now social exclusion.[41]

The standard answer to the combination of skill shortages with surplus unskilled labour has been education, vocational training, adjustment assistance, and flexibility (as well as, of course, raising the total level of demand). But experience has shown that these have worked for the bright, well-motivated; but for the not-so-bright and not committed to the work ethic they have reinforced a sense of failure. As Ronald Dore has said: "Vocational training is an area where Say's law does not operate; supply emphatically does not create its own demand."[42] A careful and thorough evaluation of government training programmes in the USA concludes that the most successful results were registered for adult women. Adult men and youth do not seem to have benefited. The authors conclude that "[t]here remains...a lack of compelling evidence that skills-building activities have actually enhanced skills that are of value to employers."[43]

The new technologies in information and communication and their global spread have brought with them learning-ability-related inequality. The new underclass, consisting of the least educated, older workers and some women, should be our concern both from motives of sympathy and social solidarity, and from the threat their existence poses for society: rise in crime, drug use, etc. The human costs of long-term unemployment go beyond the loss of income and production, and include lack of recognition, divorce, mental illness, violence in the home, suicide, and other social costs.

Unemployment can also be caused by low-cost imports from the low-income countries. Even though the percentage of these imports is small, they occur in the labour-intensive sectors, and firms often displace labour by capital in order to remain competitive.

To sum up, the causes of unemployment in the OECD countries are global competition in the form of imports from low-wage countries and export of jobs by multinational firms, often through outsourcing, lack of basic skills in an age of high and rapidly advancing technology, slow growth of demand, paying people to be unemployed instead of

---

[41] Ronald Dore has written illuminatingly about these problems. See for example his comments on Lord Dahrendorf's lecture (1996).

[42] Dore (1996).

[43] Daniel Friedlander, David H. Greenberg and Philip K. Robins (1997), p.1848.

helping them back to work, inflationary wage leap-frogging, immigrant workers, and the entry of women into the workforce. How much unemployment is due to each of these causes has been the subject of a considerable debate.

Even though few would maintain today that a higher level of effective demand (e.g. through public investment), even if buttressed with an incomes policy to keep inflation under control, is the whole answer to "structural unemployment," it would surely make a contribution to reducing unemployment as part of a package. And it is not at all clear that our society cannot use plenty of health workers, nurses, child care workers, special-education teachers, home health care aides, manicurists, gardeners, plumbers, sweepers, protectors and restorers of the environment, valet parkers, janitors, cleaners, waiters, salesmen, physical training instructors, musicians, designers, and other service workers who do not need the high and scarce skills demanded by modern technology and whose services cannot be replaced by either computers or imported low-cost goods from low-income countries (though imported low-cost labour from poor countries should be welcomed). In fact, it is precisely for these jobs which cannot be replaced by computers that the demand is likely to increase in the future. The Bureau of Labor Statistics considers many of these jobs as likely to be the fastest growing over the next decade. Many of these jobs are, however, in the currently despised and neglected public sector and may call for even more despised higher taxation. They are also often ill-paid and not recognised as valuable. We need to change our valuation of such work and should guarantee minimum standards of reward for them.

In ex-socialist countries the reason for unemployment is the need to close down inefficient, over-manned public enterprises and those that produced for the military, and to relocate labour to more efficient activities and produce goods in demand. The breakdown of institutions is largely responsible for the large amount of unemployment, often not registered as such.

In developing countries the causes of unemployment are multiple. Above all the following factors account for it:

1. the absence of cooperating factors such as capital, materials, management, skills, infrastructure, etc;

2. obstacles in the form of absence of institutions such as labour exchanges, credit banks, training schemes, security of land tenure, and systems of wide-spread land ownership;
3. inhibitions and aspirations in attitudes to work, that prevent some workers from accepting certain jobs, so that unemployment is accompanied by labour shortages;
4. barriers to efficient work resulting from low levels of living, such as inadequate nutrition, health and education;
5. the low level of demand in the industrial countries for the exports of the developing countries, the result partly of slow growth, partly of technical progress, and partly of trade barriers; and
6. the policies of the developing countries that often over-price labour, underprice capital, and overvalue exchange rates. These policies stand in the way of full and efficient labour utilisation.[44]

Another set of circumstances prevalent in many low-income countries is the existence of conditions in which higher wages enable workers to be better nourished and therefore to become more productive. Absence of malnutrition increases their alertness and their physical strength, and reduces absenteeism from illness. Individual firms are not in a position to decide to pay these higher wages, partly because they may not be able to hold on to their more productive labour force and may be financing only the profits of others, and partly because they may not recognise the profit opportunities and the economy of high wages. When factory legislation was introduced in England in the 19th century, English industrialists predicted that the higher costs would ruin British industry. In fact it flourished.

---

[44] David Card and Alan Krueger have found that for some fast food restaurants in New Jersey and neighbouring Pennsylvania (as a control group) higher minimum wages have led to *higher* employment. These findings led to considerable controversy. David Card and Alan B. Krueger (1995). Better data collected later supported their original research as reported in *the Wall Street Journal*, December 23 1997 and published in a working paper by Princeton University. David Neumark of Michigan State University and William Wascher of the Federal Reserve Board have produced their own data, attempting to refute the thesis.

5. Globalisation and income distribution

Globalisation goes with opening up countries, expanding international trade and finance, and outward-looking policies generally. How does globalisation affect income distribution within rich and poor countries and between them? Theoretical arguments suggest that expanding trade in manufactured goods and services between the South and the North reduces inequality between skilled workers and semiskilled workers (with primary and some secondary education) who can find jobs, in the South, while increasing it in the North.[45] This is so because exporting more from the South raises the demand for, and the wages of, workers with basic education relative to those with higher skills in the South. (The exception to this is where the abandonment of minimum wage legislation and the weakening of trade unions and colonially inherited wage levels as a result of international competition lowers the wages of factory workers and public employees.) The reverse is true in the North where skill differentials in wages can be expected to widen and semiskilled workers to suffer a reduction in wages, or with sticky wages unemployment among the semiskilled to grow. The relatively abundant factor gains from opening up trade, the relatively scarce one loses. These losses inevitably accompany the gains from trade. Those who hail the great gains from trade liberalisation ought to accept that there are also these losses. The gains depend on a reallocation of resources which increases the demand for some kinds of labour, while reducing it for others.

Dani Rodrik has shown that in addition to the lowering of demand for low-skilled labour, there is a flattening of the demand

---

[45] Adrian Wood (1994). A research project at the Center for Economic Policy Analysis at the New School for Social Research suggests that unemployment or growing inequality are also a function of the lower growth rates comnpared with the 1950s and 1960s and that institutional characteristics of the labour market are as important as skill levels in determining the pattern of job loss. See *CEPA News (1997)*, p. 2.

curve, an increase in the elasticity of demand, as a result of outsourcing, trade and foreign investment. This in turn has the effects of (1) putting a larger share of the cost of improvements in work conditions and benefits on workers; (2) increasing the volatility of wages and hours worked for the low-skilled in response to shocks in labour demand or productivity; and (3) weakening their bargaining power. These effects may well be more important than the lowering of demand. "[W]orkers now find themselves in an environment in which they can more easily be 'exchanged' for workers in other countries. For those who lack the skills to make themselves hard to replace, the result is greater insecurity and a more precarious existence." Lower wages would also account for the absence of a large increase in trade.[46]

Partly as a result of the greater international mobility of capital, tax rates on capital have tended to decrease in the rich countries since the early 1980s, while tax rates on labour have generally tended to increase. And while the need for social spending (unemployment insurance, pensions, family benefits, adjustment assistance) has increased, the amount has shrunk as a ratio of national income.

Empirical evidence confirms growing wage inequality or unemployment in the North. Trade liberalisation raises the wages of skilled workers in rich countries, where they are relatively abundant, and lowers those of unskilled workers. This will provide some incentives to reduce the supply of unskilled labour and to acquire the required skills. The government can assist in this process by improving training and education. Subsidies to the unskilled (tax cuts, wage supplementation, improved public services) or their employers help in the interim. Though it has been argued that this would delay the acquisition of skills, low wages and unemployment are an obstacle to skill acquisition. Though they provide an incentive to acquire skills, they deprive people of the means to do so. The net effect of subsidised wages for the unskilled, particularly if combined with their and their children's education, is likely to be positive.[47] The widening inequality in the rich countries has been aggravated by immigration of low-skilled workers. Both forces were also at work in the globalisation process before 1914.[48]

---

[46] Dani Rodrik (1997) pp. 26-27.
[47] Adrian Wood (1995) p. 78.
[48] Jeffrey G. Williamson (1997), pp. 117-135.

The prediction of the theory that wage differentials in the developing countries are narrowed does not hold for all countries in the South. Changes similar to those observed in the North appear to have occurred in some developing countries. In Mexico, for example, the difference between a typical university-educated worker's pay and that of an unskilled worker rose by a third between 1987 and 1993. Similar differentials are observed in Brazil, Argentina, Chile, Uruguay, Colombia, Costa Rica, Thailand, and the Philippines.[49]

There are several possible explanations for this. First, other factors than trade liberalisation have influenced wage differentials, among them economic growth, capital accumulation, new technologies, inflation, recession, inflows of foreign capital, etc. Second, the theory assumes the same technological production functions in all countries and absence of capital mobility. In fact, reduced trade barriers and additional foreign investment may bring in more new capital equipment and new technology, which tends to raise the demand for skilled workers Many of the activities that are complementary to exports and direct foreign investment, such as banking, finance, insurance, accounting and other services, demand a lot of skilled labour. Third, some developing countries, particularly the more advanced among them, have much larger skilled workforces than others. The impact of trade liberalisation on them will therefore be similar to that on the rich countries of the North. With China, Indonesia and other large low-income countries entering world markets for labour-intensive manufactured products the comparative advantage of the middle-income countries has shifted to goods requiring medium skills. The low-skilled workers in these countries under the new division of labour among developing countries suffer now the same fate that similar workers had previously suffered in the high-income countries. Unfortunately, only a few countries collect figures on wage differentials and the figures are not available to make these comparisons over a wide range.

The rise in demand for skilled labour in the North is only partly due to increased manufactured imports or their threat from foreign countries. Another important reason is technical progress and organisational change that save semiskilled labour. There has been considerable controversy as to how much is due to each of these

---

[49] See *The Economist* (1996), p.74 and the reference there to Donald Robbins (1996).

forces.[50] Those who attribute little of the growing inequality to trade
have argued that the developing countries account only for a small
proportion of national income, and that the prices of labour-intensive
goods (garments, textiles, footwear, etc.) have not fallen relative to
those of skill-intensive ones. But technology and trade are, to some
extent, interdependent. In order to meet foreign competition, firms have
to introduce new technology, and new technology makes them more
competitive. On the other hand, a large part of technical progress is
independent of trade. Cheap energy and the first wave of automation
eliminated most of the manual jobs. Electronics is now eliminating
routine white-collar jobs. But technical progress also saves some types
of skilled, even highly skilled, labour, as "Deep Blue," IBM's chess-
playing super-computer demonstrates. It proved itself a fair match to
Garry Kasparov. Activities that can be reduced to simple rules, even if
these may give rise to apparently infinite possibilities, are targets for
automation.[51]

In more recent work, Adrian Wood, the main proponent of the
view that it is trade, not technology, that has increased the differentials
in the rich countries, has written that we should distinguish between the
rise in demand for skilled labour in the last two decades and the
acceleration in the growth rate of demand between pre-1980 and post-
1980. His answer to the first question, like that of most other
economists, is "mainly technology." But his answer to the second
question is "mainly trade."[52] He writes: "My belief is that most
(between two-thirds and three-quarters) of the *rise* in the relative
demand for skilled labour during the past two decades was caused by
the same force that had propelled it upward over the previous century,
namely skill-based technical change, loosely defined to include factoral
and sectoral biases in production methods, product innovation and
shifts in the composition of final demand. At the same time, however, I
believe that most of the *acceleration* in the growth rate of the relative
demand for skilled labour in the past two decades above its trends of

---

[50] In spite of the differences over what caused rising wage inequalities, both sides in the debate
reject protectionism as the correct policy response. Education and income redistribution are
favoured by both sides instead.

[51] It was reported in *The New York Times* (1996) that a computer has been able to solve a
mathematical theorem that involved creative thinking, going beyond the application of rules.

[52] Adrian Wood (1998) pp. 1463-1482.

the previous few decades, and hence the rise in labour market inequalities, was caused by globalisation."[53]

Another cause of the decline in the demand for, and the wages of, semi-skilled labour in the advanced countries is outsourcing of activities that require relatively unskilled labour.[54] "In fact, the whole distinction between 'trade' versus 'technology' becomes suspect when we think of corporations shifting activities overseas. The increase in outsourcing activity during the 1980s was in part related to improvements in communication technology and the speed with which product quality and design can be monitored, which was in turn related to the use of computers.[55]

The income differentials between semiskilled and unskilled workers are expected to widen in the South, but unskilled workers are to be found mainly in agriculture, not in manufacturing, which requires a minimum of skills. Where unskilled workers are plentiful, the country does not export many manufactures. The situation in countries that export primary goods, often among the poorest, is different.[56] Mineral exports tend to increase inequality, because they require little unskilled labour and the ownership of minerals is usually highly concentrated. Reductions in inequality there depend on the government capturing a large share of the rent of the mining companies and spending it on the poor. The effect of agricultural exports on distribution depends on the pattern of land ownership. Where exports are produced on plantations or privately owned large farms, their expansion will tend to increase inequality, unless the workers are organised in powerful trade unions. If the increased exports are produced on small farms, worked by the owners and their families, inequality will tend to be reduced.

This analysis has several limitations. The Stolper-Samuelson theorem predicts that the absolute reward of the scarce factor will fall under free trade. In the present context, absolute real wages of unskilled and semi-skilled workers in the North would fall. The mechanism by which this result is brought about is the reduction in the relative price of the unskilled- and semi-skilled-intensive product in international trade. But the assumptions on which the theorem is true are very restrictive. It may be more realistic to assume that relative

---

[53] Adrian Wood (1998) p. 1465.

[54] See Robert C. Feenstra (1998) pp. 31-50.

[55] Robert C. Feenstra (1998) p. 41.

[56] See Adrian Wood (1994) p. 244 and François Bourgignon and Christian Morrison (1989) pp. 273-81 quoted in Adrian Wood (1994).

wages of low-skilled workers fall. We are then concerned with inequality, which many would regard as an evil, rather than with absolute poverty, which the same people and many more would regard as a greater evil. In an expanding economy, it would not be surprising to find that some groups move ahead of others; and this would not matter, indeed should be welcomed, as long as there is not an increase in absolute poverty, and as long as those left behind at first would eventually catch up with or overtake those ahead. Development means a shift in the structure of production. Employment in industry and services increases, while that in agriculture relatively and, beyond a certain point absolutely, drops. Wages in industry and services are higher than incomes in agriculture. The result is an increase in inequality, but most workers are better off and no one is worse off.

Anthony Atkinson has criticized the analysis of widening wage differentials in terms of supply and demand only, which he calls the Transatlantic Consensus, on the ground that its model is too simple.[57] The rise in inequality is neither universal in the OECD countries nor of the same extent everywhere; nor does it continue consistently, increases are followed by plateaus. The two-country, two-factor model (skilled and unskilled labour) can be misleading. He also criticizes it for neglecting the role of conventions and social norms. Whatever the explanation, however, Atkinson rightly says that rising inequality is not inevitable but can be corrected by redistribution through fiscal policies and social transfers.

Ravi Kanbur has pointed out that different assumptions about market structure and power would lead to different conclusions.[58] The implicit framework of the neoclassical view is that of a competitive market structure of many small agents interacting with each other without market power. Opening trade would, on these assumptions, benefit the relatively abundant factor in poor countries, which is unskilled labour. But if markets are segmented, because of poor infrastructure or because of the monopoly power of middlemen and money lenders, the theory does not apply. Unskilled labour may lose even in poor countries.

Similarly with capital mobility. Even neoclassical economists have admitted the case for some restrictions on the flow of portfolio capital since the financial crises of the 1990ies, but not for investment

---

[57] Anthony B. Atkinson (1999).
[58] Ravi Kanbur (2001)

capital. The advocates of free investment capital mobility argue that it is inconsistent to say that it hurts both the workers in the receiving and those in the sending countries. But it could be that increased mobility increases the bargaining power of capital in both sets of countries. When labour bargains with capital over wages and employment in not completely competitive markets it could then be that workers are worse off relatively to capital in both sets of countries.

Another limitation of the analysis is that it is concerned only with different kinds of wages (and often only urban wages) and not with other incomes, such as profits and rents (except for the brief discussion of exporters of primary goods). There is much evidence that globalisation has led to growing inequalities between incomes from labour and those from capital. For example, in the USA between 1974 and 1994 families in the upper 5 per cent of income distribution enjoyed an average annual gain in income of 1.2 per cent; those in the bottom fifth saw their incomes shrink. In 1999 the richest 2.7 million Americans, the top 1 per cent, have the same income after taxes as the bottom 100 million. This ratio has more than doubled since 1977, when the top 1 per cent had as much as the bottom 49 million.[59] J. P. Morgan said that no chief executive officer should earn more than twenty times what his workers are paid. In 1998 the C.E.O.s of big companies in the USA received as "compensation," on average, four hundred and nineteen times the earnings of a typical production workers.[60]

So far we have considered the impact of globalisation and trade on domestic income distribution. The analysis of international income distribution has undergone a shift. In the 70s, during the debate on the New International Economic Order, it was said that rich countries benefit at the expense of poor countries. Today, the complaint is that poor countries attract industry and services by their low-cost labour and that the North suffers, as a result, from unemployment and low wages.

One can approach international income distribution between countries by examining the impact of multinational corporations, whose role in the globalisation process has enormously increased. Foreign capital, know-how, enterprise, management and marketing are highly mobile internationally and are combined with the plentiful but internationally much less mobile domestic semi-skilled labour. One set of factors (enterprise, management, knowledge and capital) are in

---

[59] Data from the Congressional Budget Office reported in *The New York Times* (1999) p.16.

[60] This includes stock grants and option packages. John Cassidy (1999) p. 32.

relatively *inelastic* supply in *total*, but if not dependent on local natural capital such as mines or plantations, easily moved around the world in response to small differential rewards. They are, therefore, in highly *elastic* supply to *any particular country*. The other factor, labour, is in *highly elastic supply* domestically in labour-surplus economies, but relatively *immobile* across frontiers. The situation is aggravated by the fact that if the workers produce manufactured goods that can be produced anywhere in the world, their labour is also in elastic demand, so that combining to raise their wages would lead only to unemployment. The situation is equivalent to one in which plentiful semi-skilled labour itself, rather than the product of labour, is exported. The surplus of the product of labour over the wage, resulting from the cooperation of other factors, in less elastic supply, accrues to foreigners. The differential international and internal elasticities of supply in response to differential rewards, and the monopoly rents entering the reward of these factors, have important implications for the international distribution of gains from investment.

Since the firms operate in oligopolistic and oligopsonistic markets, cost advantages are not necessarily passed on to consumers in lower prices or to workers in higher wages, and the profits then accrue to the parent firms. The operation of this type of international specialisation depends upon the continuation of substantial wage differentials (hence trade unions must be weak in the host country so that low wage costs are maintained), continuing access to the markets of the parent companies (hence stronger political pressure from importing interests than from domestic producers displaced by the low-cost components and processes, including trade unions in the rich importing countries) and continuing permission by host countries to operate with minimum taxes, tariffs and bureaucratic regulation.

The packaged or complete nature of the contribution of the transnational enterprise, usually claimed as its characteristic blessing, is then the cause of the unequal international division of gains. If the package broke, or leaked, some of the rents and monopoly rewards would spill over into the host country. But if it is secured tightly, only the least scarce and weakest factor in the host country derives a limited income from the operations of the transnational firm.

These tendencies can be and have been offset in some cases by several factors. The developing country can use its bargaining power to extract a share of these rents (though any one country's attempt to tax footloose multinational corporations suffers from the Prisoner's

Dilemma situation) and apply them to social services or public works for the poor; or investment in human capital can create domestically some of the scarce factors and skim off some of the rents. This has occurred in the more successful developing countries. This is, indeed, what development is about. As the developing country increases the domestic value-added in its exports, its growth rate rises. This is one of the forces making for globalisation. It also shows the limits of the conventional distinction between import substitution and export orientation. For the increased domestic value-added is a form of import substitution, while the increase in exports represents at the same time export orientation.

Now assume that the package can be unbundled and that some of its components, such as high skills, can be transferred to the developing country. Consider a model in which two types of service have to be combined, one highly skilled, the other less skilled, such as air transport. The providers of the skilled service, say pilots, are in relatively scarce total supply,[61] but highly mobile between countries in response to financial incentives. Only because people are tied by language, culture, family and friends can there be permanent differences in the salaries of these pilots. On a clear day, an airline pilot can see the world, while the scruffy people who clear the ashtrays and remove the trash of the aeroplanes on the ground are wholly earth-bound. The semiskilled factor, ground personnel, is in highly elastic local supply, but immobile between countries. Other examples are transnational advertising, hotel chains, tourist enclaves, etc. The result will be that pilots will earn large rents, while ground personnel will get the bare minimum wage. Any country, even a very poor one, wishing to have an airline, will have to pay its pilots not very much less than the high international salaries or it will lose them. An egalitarian domestic incomes policy will be impossible, not so much because of the brain drain, the loss to foreign countries of trained professional manpower, but in order to counteract the brain drain and to prevent that loss. Both international and domestic inequalities will have to be large. Once again, partial international integration (that of the skilled and professional people) leads to national disintegration. Increasingly, there

---

[61] According to an article in the *Wall Street Journal* of June 4 1998 the American demand for pilots is "soaring" and "going sky high." An editorial in the same paper of July 27 2000 is headed "Short on Pilots."

are First Worlds to be found within Third World countries, Belgiums within Indias, or Belindias as this situation has been called.

Members of the élites in the low-income countries have their medical and surgical treatment in the advanced capital cities of the North. They send their children to the schools in the North. They take their vacations there, do their shopping there, and visit relatives who have settled there. They invest their capital on the stock exchanges of the rich countries. As a result, they have no interest in improving the medical, educational and economic facilities in their own countries. Local "capacity building" is not part of their agenda. Partial international integration leads to national disintegration.

To sum up, the frequently adopted notion that globalisation is the same as international integration is not tenable. There are at least six reasons for why partial international integration leads to national disintegration.

1. Downsizing, restructuring, "delayering," and reengineering (not words that are part of my active vocabulary) have reduced the demand for low-skilled workers in the rich and middle-income countries and kept the wages of those who succeeded in keeping their jobs low.
2. Preventing the brain drain in developing countries makes egalitarian incomes policies impossible. To prevent the professional and skilled people from leaving they have to be paid something not too far out of line with their pay in the rich countries.
3. Tax revenues to pay for social services have been reduced, though the need for them has increased.
4. The élites in the low-income countries are opting out of national commitments and take as their reference group the élites in the advanced countries. This leads to the neglect of essential social services like education and health.
5. The culture of the élites is global and estranged from the culture of the local people.
6. The tendency for minorities to break away from their country and form independent nations, resulting in the proliferation of states, can be explained by their desire to participate directly in the benefits of globalisation.

Globalisation has led to polarisation. The ratio of the income of the top 20 per cent of the world's population to the income of the bottom 20 per cent rose from 30 to 1 in 1960 to 78 to 1 in 1994. And extreme poverty and misery is the fate of the fastest growing segment of the poor population in almost every country.

6. The poor and globalisation

The Grameen Bank of Bangladesh is frequently and rightly upheld as a wonderful model of how to lift the poor out of poverty. It lends small sums mainly to poor rural women (who spend it on the welfare of their children) to build fish ponds or to buy dairy cows and rice-husking machines; it uses peer pressure in small groups of five to achieve repayments; it is a non-governmental, and therefore flexible, organization although it derives some of its funds from the government; it teaches people to help themselves; and it has a spectacularly good repayments record: 94 to 99 per cent have been cited. It fosters enterprise rather than dependence and is self-sustaining. Its latest achievement is to introduce cell phones into 300 villages, each telephone being owned by a Grameen borrower, the "telephone lady." Two independent companies were formed, one for profit with Telenor of Norway as one of its partners, the other not for profit.

The Grameen Bank started with a personal loan by Muhammad Yunus, its founder, of $ 27 to 42 poor people in his village to free them from the slavery to moneylenders and middlemen.[62] The model of the Grameen Bank has been replicated around the world, including in many rich countries. Its point is that the burden of screening and enforcement is transferred from the lending institution to borrowers' groups. This obviously reduces costs. A disadvantage is that small groups of borrowers are less able to bear risks than credit institutions. But reduced moral hazard and reduced adverse selection, resulting from this method, may override the higher social costs from the wrong party bearing the risks. But it is less widely known that it is difficult to find enough bank workers to process the loans, that the turnover of these workers is high and more are leaving than re-entering, that the credit extended represents only a tiny proportion of total credit (all NGOs provide only 0.6 per cent of total credit), and, most striking of all, that some of these record high repayments are made by borrowing

---

[62] Muhammad Yunus (1999).

from the village usurer. This can be regarded either as a victory or as a failure of the Grameen Bank.

Former President of the World Bank, Barber Conable, provoked Yunus by claiming, wrongly, that the Bank had given financial support to the Grameen Bank. Three times at the same broadcast session Yunus had to deny, in ever stronger terms, that his bank had ever accepted money from the Word Bank (though later the Grameen Trust was accepting money from the Bank). Yunus does not like the way the Bank conducts its business. He also told Conable, who was bragging about employing the best minds in the world, that hiring smart economists does not necessarily translate into policies and programmes that benefit the poor. Yunus is highly critical of most donor agencies.

An NGO like the Grameen Bank cannot replace governments or commercial credit. Instead, its function should be to exert political pressure on the government to change its policies, to pioneer models that can be replicated and to work with the government. Only 1.4 million people were served by the Grameen Bank out of a population of 120 million, about 1%. It is sometimes claimed that the NGO works without and against the government. Yunus does not claim this, but he is for minimal government. In fact the Grameen Bank relies heavily on the government. In 1990 the Bangladesh government contributed 60% to its capital.

Not all poor communities can rely on the close ties between groups of women. The urban poor often do not know their neighbours well enough to act as guarantors for them. In the shanty towns of Africa and Latin America what is called "stepped lending" replaces group finance. A borrower puts up a little money of her own. The bank lends her about the same amount. If she repays promptly, she can raise a larger loan. The better her credit record becomes, the more she can borrow. The place of peer pressure in the village is taken by the promise of more credit.

The impact of modern technologies such as cell telephones or the Internet on traditional, poor societies that had been closed off from the world is changing the relations of people to one another, both within and between countries The old power structures are undermined as previously oppressed and dependent women get independent access to money and power. Projects bring the Web to communities as varied as the reindeer-herding Sami of Scandinavia and northern Russia, the aboriginal peoples of the Northwest Territories in Canada, the ethnic minorities of Burma and native Hawaiians. Traditional cultures have often been romanticized and it is important to recognize and preserve their valuable features. But they can also be oppressive, especially for women, and modern technology can contribute to changing this. Clearly, the Internet is no substitute for food, health services and education, but it can improve poor people's access to them, once their basic needs are met.

As a result of the spread of information technology and democracy, not only will the poor know more about conditions in the rich countries, but their voice will be heard more loudly there. Their governments will stir up trouble and may embark on military adventures if world poverty in the midst of plenty persists.

7. Government and open economies

Most economists would expect globalisation to have gone hand in hand with a shrinkage of government. They would expect the size of government to be smaller the more open the economy.[63] This is so for two reasons. First, liberal trade policies tend to go together with a preference for markets and therefore less government. Second, globalisation has made government monetary and fiscal policies less effective. This would be expected to lead to smaller government. Yet, Dani Rodrik has shown that the scope of government has been larger, not smaller, in economies that have taken greater advantage of world markets. There is a positive correlation between openness, as measured by the share of trade in GDP, and the scope of government, as measured by the share of government expenditure in GDP. Small, open economies like Sweden, Austria, Switzerland, Belgium, Luxembourg, and the Netherlands have large governments. Rodrik suggests that the explanation is to be found in the role of government as an insulator against external shocks, as a kind of insurance against external risk, a way of alleviating market dislocations. He proposes two measures for external risk: the volatility of the terms of trade and the concentration by products of exports (the ratio of one or two products to total exports). It could also be argued according to the "new" growth theory that, challenged by fiercer competition, governments spend more on public goods like education, R&D, and infrastructure.

Rodrik's hypothesis depends on three presumptions. The first is that increases in trade lead to greater external risk; the second that increases in external risk lead to greater income volatility; and the third that a larger share of government purchases in GDP reduces income volatility. The first presumption may be doubted. Diversified international trade (diversified by goods, services, countries of origin

[63] This section draws on a paper by Dani Rodrik (1996). See also Geoffrey Garrett and Peter Lange (1995) pp. 627-55 and Geoffrey Garrett (1995) pp. 657-87. I am grateful to James Robinson for having drawn my attention to these articles.

and countries of destination) can be a good way of insuring against risks. For example, a country depending wholly on domestic food production is in great trouble if its domestic harvest fails; or one depending on domestic coal for energy if its miners go on strike. If coal mining is in the public sector, government ownership presents greater risks than a diversified policy of importing fuel. Self-reliance is sometimes confused with self-sufficiency, but the latter can be at the expense of the former. But it is true that certain shocks, such as that of the oil price increases in the 1970s, are the result of dependence on international trade.

Rodrik eliminates other possible explanations of the positive link between openness and government, such as that small countries are both more open and tend to have higher government expenditures, and that European countries have both larger government sectors and are more open owing to being members of the European Union. His conclusion that globalisation may well require big, not small, government is in line with my argument elsewhere that markets and pricism do not call for state minimalism, but for an active, interventionist state.[64]

Views for globalisation versus separatism and about government versus non-intervention can be put into four rubrics:

		Separatism	Globalisation
Government Intervention (national global)	*and*	Nationalistic dirigistes	This paper's position
Laissez-faire		Nationalistic (classical) liberals (Ross Perot, Patrick Buchanan, Jörg Haider)	Global (classical) liberals

In spite of the anti-big-government rhetoric, government has not shrunk in the advanced countries. In 1979, the year Mrs. Thatcher became Prime Minister, the share of government expenditure in British GNP was 38.0%; by the end of her term, in 1990, it was 38.2%. In the USA, it rose during Reagan's Presidency from 33.7% in 1980 to 36.1% in 1988. Between 1980 and 1991 the share rose in all Western countries except in the Netherlands where it had already reached 52.5% in

---

[64] Paul Streeten (1993) pp. 1281-1298.

1980.[65] And in spite of the rapid growth of trade, protection remains entrenched in the Common Agricultural Policy of the European Union and in tariff and non-tariff barriers to trade in many rich countries.

---

[65] World Bank (1993).

8. Technology and institutions

We are suffering from a lag of institutions behind technology. The revolutions in the technologies of transport, travel, communications and information have unified and shrunk the globe,[66] but our organisation into nation states dates back to the Peace of Westphalia in 1648, to the American constitution and the French revolution in 1789, to the 19th century when first Italy (1861) and then Germany (1871) were unified, and to the breakup of empires into nation states after World War I. And while technology marches on to organise the world into a single unit, nations are becoming more numerous and more acutely self-conscious. Or, to put it in Marxian terms, there is a contradiction between the forces of production, which have been globalised, and the relations of production, which reflect the nation states.

Biotechnology and materials technology offer considerable promise, but it is the micro-electronic revolution in information and communication technology that is most relevant to globalisation. Few manufacturing and service industries have remained untouched by the application of the microprocessor to new products and new processes.[67] Communication, information and the media have been transformed by it. Advances in telecommunications and information technology are expanding the boundaries of tradability in services - the fastest-growing component of trade and foreign direct investment.

When the nation states were founded, the city states and the feudalism that preceded them had become too small for the scale of operations required by the Industrial Revolution. The political institution therefore was adapted to the new industrial technology, to the roads, railways and canals. The nation state was then a progressive

---

[66] This does not mean that people have necessarily benefited from this technological globalisation. Economic and technical progress translates at the global level even less than at the national level automatically into human wellbeing.

[67] Charles Oman (undated).

institution. But I am not a technological determinist. The adaptation of institutions to technology is not an inevitable process. The Middle Ages had, for example, lost the Roman technology about roads, baths, aquaeducts and amphitheatres, and these were allowed to fall into disrepair. But now the nation state, with its insistence on full sovereignty, has become, at least in certain respects, an obstacle to further progress. It has landed us in several Prisoners' Dilemma situations: each nation acts in its own perceived rational self-interest, and the result is that every country is worse off. It pays each nation to pursue this mutually destructive course, whether others do likewise or not. To overcome such destructive outcomes calls for a high degree of trust, moral motivation (even if, as in the case of the Prisoners' Dilemma, it is honour among thieves), cooperation or compulsion.

I shall not discuss the desirability or the feasibility of a world government. If it ever were to come about, it would probably be the result of a trend we are already beginning to observe. What I have in mind are technically clearly defined areas of international cooperation, or delegation of these functions upwards to a global body. The Universal Postal Union, established in 1875, may serve as a model.

Common interests and conflicts are running nowadays across national boundaries and against other interests in the same country. The European farmers are in conflict with the European industrialists and the public and outside competitive producers, who have to pay for the Common Agricultural Policy. The advanced countries' textile manufacturers are aligned in the Multifibre Arrangement against Third World textile exporters and consumers in their own countries. A proposed alliance between Boeing and Airbus to produce a new 800-seat super jumbo-jet would create a supra-national monopoly that would raise questions of competition versus innovation and may be against the interests of consumers.[68] The nation state has shown itself to be an inappropriate level at which such issues can be resolved.

At the international level, prisoners' dilemma outcomes move the world economy away from a more to a less efficient allocation of resources. There exist, therefore, potential gains, by moving back to more efficient allocations. According to Coase's theorem, in the absence of transaction costs and with full information, a legal framework and well-defined property rights, it pays each state to reach agreements with other states to avoid, by compensation payments, this

---

[68] See Sylvia Ostry (1995).

damage and make all better off than they would have been in the outcome of the Prisoners' Dilemma.[69] For example, the US emits acid rain to Canada. If the damage is greater than the benefits to the USA, Canada could offer compensation to the US for relinquishing the emission of sulfur dioxide, the chief component in acid rain, and still be better off than it would be in accepting the acid rain; or, if the benefits are greater than the damage, the US can offer compensation to Canada for accepting the acid rain and still be better off than it would have been, had it been prevented from inflicting the damage. But as we all know to our regret, we are far away from outcomes according to Coase's theorem, although we are not always at the other end of the spectrum, the Prisoners' Dilemma. Coase's theorem remains useful, in spite of its unrealistic assumptions, in drawing our attention to the fact that there are unexploited mutual profit opportunities when prisoners' dilemma situations arise. I obviously do not wish to say that compensation always, or even often, ought to be paid. The losers, such as the English landlords after the repeal of the Corn Laws in 1846, may not have deserved to be compensated; or, even if they did deserve it, the administrative costs and the losses from imposing taxes to finance the compensation might have been so large as to make the compensation uneconomic. But the fact that it *could* be paid draws our attention to potential unexploited gains.

Add to the Prisoners' Dilemma the free rider problem, according to which each country relies on others to bear the costs of arrangements that benefit everybody. As a result, international or global public goods, such as peace, an open trading system, including standards of weights and measures, freedom of the seas, well defined property rights, international stability, a working monetary system, or conservation of the global environment, are undersupplied, while public bads, such as wars, pollution, diseases and poverty are oversupplied. The situation has been described in parables and similes such as the tragedy of the commons, social traps, the isolation paradox, etc.

Under the present system there are apparent gains to uncoordinated action. It pays any one country to put up protectionist

---

[69] I am indebted to Michael Lipton's analysis of the relation between Prisoners' Dilemma and Coase's Theorem in a different context. See Michael Lipton (1985) pp. 49-109. M. J. Farrell has shown that the Coase theorem, according to which individuals could resolve problems of externalities and public goods as well as governments provided that property rights are assigned, is not correct. See M.J. Farrell (1987) pp. 113-129.

barriers, whether others do so or not; to build up its arms promises security to any one country, whether others do so or not; any one country can to its advantage pollute the common air and the oceans, whether others do so or not. It pays any one country to attract capital from abroad by tax incentives, whether others do so or not, thereby eroding the tax bases of all countries. These mutually damaging and ultimately self-damaging and possibly self-destructive actions can be avoided, in the absence of self-restraint, only by either a dominant world power imposing the restraints, or by cooperation or, most effectively of all, by delegation of some decisions to a transnational authority, with the power to enforce restraint or contributions.

The ranking of preferences with respect to, say, contributing to a common public good by each country is the following:

1. My country does not contribute while others do. (Free rider, defection of one.)
2. My country contributes together with others. (Cooperation.)
3. No country contributes. (Prisoners' Dilemma outcome.)
4. My country contributes while no other country does. (Sucker.)

Behaviour by each according to 1, or the fear of 4, leads to outcome 3. Although outcome 2 is preferred to 3, we end up with the less preferred situation 3, unless either rewards and penalties, or autonomous cooperative motivations lead to 2. Incentives and expectations must be such as to rule out outcomes 4 and 1, so that if I (or you) contribute, I (or you) will not end up a sucker. In the absence of such motivations, the result is that such global public goods as peace, monetary stability, absence of inflation, expansion of output and employment, an open world economy, environmental protection, debt relief, raw material conservation, poverty reduction and world development will be undersupplied.

It has been shown that iterative games of the Prisoners' Dilemma type lead to non-destructive outcomes.[70] The partners learn and adopt mutually beneficial strategies. I have already said that we find ourselves in between the two extremes of Prisoners' Dilemmas and Coase's outcomes. For several reasons it is harder to reach cooperative agreements in international transactions than in others, in which mutual trust and a sense of duty play stronger parts. First, there are now many

---

[70] R. Axelrod (1984).

states, nearly 200, and large numbers make agreements more difficult and defection more likely. Second, we do not have a world government or a global police force that could enforce agreements. Third, change is rapid, which undermines the basis of stability on which agreements are based. Fourth, the absence of a hegemonic power also removes the sanctions against breaking the agreement. And fifth, all these factors prevent the trust from being built up, which is an essential prerequisite for international agreements.

Examples of Prisoners' Dilemmas on the global scale are ubiquitous. Above all there was the arms race, which, though we have so far avoided a major nuclear war, has contributed to hundreds of minor wars, mostly in the Third World; then there is competitive protectionism, through which each country attempts to cast its unemployment onto others; competitive exchange rate movements, by which unemployment or inflation are exported; investment wars in which countries forgo taxation to attract a limited amount of investment; research and development wars and the resulting technological nightmares; the denial of debt relief by banks and of guarantees by governments; environmental pollution; competitive interest rate increases; over-fishing, the depletion of ocean reserves and the destruction of species are only some of the areas in which these battles are now being fought.

This problem applies not only to government policies but also to those of firms. In the field of technology, there is a tendency for firms (and countries) to move away from basic research with long-term results that are not easily appropriated and benefit other firms and other countries to short-term, commercial research, the results of which show up quickly in profits to the firm. For example, basic research into the new high-yielding varieties of wheat and rice that gave rise to the Green Revolution in the 1960s was financed neither by private firms nor by national governments but had to rely on the philanthropic Ford and Rockefeller Foundations. Their resources are clearly inadequate to research into the modern high-technology problems that will drive globalisation in the next century.

To avoid these traps, coordination, cooperation and enforcement of policies are needed. But coordination means that each country has to do things it does not want to do. The U.S. has to balance its budget in order to lower world interest rates; Germany has to grow faster, but she does not want to suck in guest workers from Turkey and Yugoslavia;

many say Japan should import more, but she does not want to hurt her domestic industries. And so on.

Even Mrs Thatcher, that archpriestess of free markets and state minimalism, in a speech to the United Nations in New York on 8th of November 1989, had come to recognize that in order to avoid global warming and coastal flooding, countries that emit carbon dioxide and other gases that trap heat in the atmosphere would have to act together, that restrictions would have to be obligatory, and their application would have to be carefully monitored. Any one country acting by itself would be at a disadvantage by having to incur the higher costs of protecting the environment.[71]

The challenge is to replace the past international orders based on dominance and dependence, like the Pax Britannica and the Pax Americana, or the disorders that showed fragmentation and lack of coordination, by a new pluralistic global order built on equality and fairness.

---

[71] *The New York Times* (1989) p. A 17.

9. Technology and the international location of industry

A question that has preoccupied scholars and policy-makers is the impact of the new technologies on the location of industries. More specifically, the question has been raised whether the revolution in electronics and the accompanying move to flexible production and the declining trend in low-wage labour costs will not deprive the developing countries of their comparative advantage in labour-intensive activities, and relocate plants back to the advanced countries. There are at least nine points to be made some of which make the prospect for the developing countries more hopeful.

1. The new technologies economise not only in labour, but also in some technical, supervisory and managerial skills, particularly those that can be encapsulated in rules and made subject to routine. These are particularly scarce in many developing countries, and their comparative advantage in these activities may therefore be restored.

2. Drawing on the experience not only of the newly industrialising countries, but of 18th and 19th century economic history, unemployment and the inability to compete with the most advanced country in an open market has been predicted repeatedly. The Luddites opposed the introduction of machinery and Friedrich List thought that Britain's advanced technology would not give Germany an opportunity to develop. The steam engine also replaced much labour, but it was absorbed in new activities. The lessons of history, so far, are that there are always some products and processes in which countries at an earlier stage of development have a comparative advantage. The product cycle is becoming shorter, but it continues to exist.

3. There is, on the other hand, possibly a lesson in the story of the Oxford College that received a large private bequest. In the senior common room the fellows were discussing how the money should

best be invested. The bursar finally said, "Well, let's invest it in property. After all, property has served us well for the last thousand years." Then the senior fellow chirped up and said, "Yes, but you know the last thousand years have been exceptional."

4. The experience of the developing countries may be compared to the man who fell out of 32nd floor, and when he reached the fourth he said, "so far, so good." There may be discontinuities in history which make the electronics revolution now underway different from anything that has happened before. It is more pervasive, it is being introduced faster, and it makes the location of work more footloose than previous technologies. But the weight of the evidence is on the other side.

5. Electronics offer hope for latecomers because they depend on classroom-learned science instead of on production engineering, such as the more old-fashioned processes, combined with more on-the-job training. Such classroom-learning is much less expensive than learning that has to be accompanied by working on expensive equipment. It is true that the science to be learned is more advanced than earlier science, but the ability of mastering it is not confined to any one group. A careful analysis of the most appropriate methods of training should therefore be high on our research agenda.

6. Flexible specialisation, which in many firms is replacing Fordist and Taylorist methods of mass production, is suited for developing countries. The method is neither capital-intensive nor foreign exchange-intensive, nor dependent on economies of large-scale production.

7. There is plenty of scope for the division of labour in the newly traded services. Developing countries can export relatively low-skilled activities such as data processing or routine programming, while rich countries can export more sophisticated services such as packaged software and engineering design. Previously untraded services have become tradable. Medical advice or education can now be sold over telecommunications networks.[72]

8. The new technology and particularly information technology, cuts the distance between grassroots producers and foreign markets. A Guatemalan weaver can have his wares displayed thousands of miles away on the Internet for marketing and information about how to improve the product. Markets are not enough but development

---

[72] Pam Woodall (1996).

institutions, marketing cooperatives, credit banks and other creative local institutions are also needed. PEOPLink is a non-governmental organisation that promotes trade and electronic communications by linking grassroots producers to global markets through the Internet.

9. The new technology, even if developed and applied in the advanced countries, will provide cheaper, better, and new imports of goods and services for the developing countries. Of course, they must be able to earn the foreign exchange to pay for these imports, but there are pointers as to how this can be done. There are also other activities, such as certain services in information technology, at which the developing countries will maintain or attain a comparative advantage.

The main conclusion to be drawn from this brief discussion is that the threat to the developing countries may not come so much from the nature of technical progress in the advanced countries, as from its pace. The greatly accelerated speed of technical change calls for a high degree of flexibility and adaptability in the developing countries. Those that cannot achieve them will lose.

The opposite fear has also been expressed and is being voiced more loudly: that the industrial countries will lose jobs to the developing countries because the new technology will make use of the lower-cost and better disciplined labour in the developing countries and this will cause massive unemployment in the industrial countries. The costs - so the argument goes - are incurred for developing the new technology in the industrial countries, while the benefits are reaped in the developing countries. Neither theory nor evidence confirms (or, for that matter, refutes) these fears. New and improved technology, if it lowers costs, must be reflected in either lower prices or higher wages or higher profits. Each one of these gives rise to higher demand, which creates new jobs. The additional exports from and the higher incomes in the developing countries also give rise to higher demand for imports, which also create more jobs in the industrial countries.

The evidence confirms this. America and Japan - the heaviest users of the new technology in manufacturing - have created more jobs than Europe. Since 1980 total employment in the USA has increased by 24 per cent, in Japan by 17 per cent, but in the European Union by less than 2 per cent. Clearly, other factors, such as greater flexibility, have also played a part. But several OECD studies have shown that the new information technology seems to be good for jobs.

But here again, there are serious problems in the transition, which call for adjustment and flexibility. As comparative advantages change continually and increasingly rapidly, these adjustments will also have to take place continually. This involves costs in financial and human terms, as people have to learn ever new skills and relocate in new places. In the extreme case, it can involve a trade policy for tramps. Few advocates of globalisation and free trade have made full allowance for these costs.

Technical progress, like trade liberalisation, involves disruption. In most other lines of advance, even in trade liberalisation, we accept the application of some form of benefit/cost calculus, but only where advances in knowledge and its technical and commercial application are concerned do we not ask questions about its social and human costs. When technological progress in synthetics knocks out lines of raw material exports on which a country is heavily dependent for foreign exchange, the costs of adjustment of the exporting country may greatly exceed the benefits to the buyers in the importing countries, quite apart from the evaluation of the distributional impact. It would then be reasonable either to ask for some form of international agreement to slow down the pace of scientific and technological progress, or to contract out of the international competitive race. The issue here is not forgoing some income for a quiet life, but by international cooperation, the avoidance of impoverishment, through deteriorating terms of trade or growing unemployment.

10. Improving international institutions and the need for institutional innovation

From the point of view of human development, which puts people on centre stage, the principle of one state one vote in the UN General Assembly (though its resolutions have only recommendatory power) cannot be justified. Respect for persons applies to equality of status enjoyed by individuals within a nation, but not to corporate entities such as states. In the United Nations context, however, it could be said that the voting rights in the Assembly compensate for the gross economic inequality manifested in international trade and the military inequality recognized in the great powers' permanent membership and veto power on the Security Council, which can reach decisions with binding force. It should also be remembered that the large and growing majority of the world's people live in the developing countries. A further justification for voting by states lies in the overriding importance of avoiding war. And the state is the institution with a monopoly of force. Yet, considerations of law and order in international relations have to be tempered by those of social justice. In civilized relations, including international relations, bargaining and negotiations do not occur in a space of pure power politics, but always appeal, openly or tacitly, to mutually accepted or acceptable values and norms.

The United Nations and its many agencies have not yet adjusted to the post-cold war era. They have been subjected to many criticisms, and numerous proposals have been made for their reform. Many have put the blame on institutional inadequacies. It is true that badly designed institutions can be formidable obstacles to reform. But even the best institutions cannot work if they are not supported by political power. In the final analysis the past defects of the United Nations agencies were not the result of institutional inadequacies, of overlaps here and gaps there, of low-level representation at important meetings, of lack of coordination, or of managerial flaws, but of lack of commitment by member governments. There were successes: the crisis in Africa, in Cambodia and in San Salvador called forth the best in the UN. In the prevention of natural disasters, in the eradication of contagious diseases and in limiting damage to the environment, the UN agencies have been quite successful. Some argue that the United Nations have been more successful in the social and economic fields than in peace-keeping, others see it the other way round.

State sovereignty, which still dominates the world order, has become inadequate and indeed dangerous. In the area of peacekeeping, the unrealistic distinction between external aggression and internal oppression should be abandoned. The predominant threat to stability is conflict within countries and not between them. There is an urgent need to strengthen international human rights. Many of the most destabilizing troubles come from within states - either because of ethnic strife or repressive measures by governments. Conditions that lead to tyranny at home sooner or later are likely to spill over into search for enemies abroad. Consider the Soviet's invasion of Hungary and Czechoslovakia, the old South African regime in Angola and Mozambique, and Iraq in Kuwait. An ounce of prevention is better than a ton of punishment. And prevention of aggression is an important task for the UN.

Urgent new claims in international coordination have been added to old ones, in the context of shrinking public expenditures. The East European countries' claims are less than those of, say, India, on grounds of poverty, and less than those of, say, Uganda, on grounds of good performance. But if the ground is the promise to move to a more peaceful world order, their claims are strong. Ideally, resources from the industrial countries to Eastern Europe and the Soviet Union should be additional to those going to the Third World. Competing claims for the countries of sub-Saharan Africa and for the industrial countries themselves are being made.

There are international institutions that work well. They never hit the headlines. They carry out their allotted tasks in a quietly effective manner. The already mentioned Universal Postal Union, founded in 1875, whose task it is to perfect postal services and to promote international collaboration, the International Telecommunication Union, the World Meteorological Association, the International Civil Aviation Organization and the World Intellectual

Property Organization have clearly and narrowly defined technical mandates, are non-politicized, and implement their tasks competently. The advantages from them are great and manifest. Their success is due largely to their covering technical, important issues.

International coordination has worked well in areas where the advantages are great and visible: the wide, though not universal, adoption of the metric system, or of Greenwich Mean Time in 1884, on which the word's time system is based, and the establishment of an international regime for containing contagious diseases.

Other international institutions have worked less well, among them the United Nations Conference on Trade and Development (UNCTAD) and the United Nations Educational, Scientific and Cultural Organization (UNESCO). Their mandates were broad, overlapping with those of other organizations, perceptions about the future, about objectives, and about which policies had which results differed, and the debates in their counsels brought in extraneous political controversies. It is from these negative experiences that some have drawn the conclusion that international cooperation is unnecessary and undesirable.

International coordination or cooperation can take different forms.[73] There can be full harmonization of policies, such as the adoption of common standards, for example the metric system. Or it can mean joint expenditures for a common purpose, such as on international air traffic control. Or it may involve submitting to agreed rules. Or it can amount to the continual exchange of information, such as that on illegal capital flight or on matters of public health. Or, as in the case of macro-economic coordination, it can involve joint decision-making on monetary, fiscal, trade and exchange rate policy.

I have given elsewhere a few illustrations of the kind of institutional innovation at the global or transnational level I have in mind that would avoid prisoners' dilemma outcomes.[74] These would realign modern technology and political institutions, would coordinate the four functions mentioned in the beginning that a global system concerned with development should fulfil, and avoid the negative-sum games to which prisoners' dilemma situations give rise.

When I propose institutional innovation here, I am not thinking of legions of international bureaucrats or gleaming, glass-plated

---

[73] See Richard N. Cooper (1985) pp. 369-370.
[74] See Paul Streeten (1995).

headquarters buildings and pools of high-paid consultants with more secretaries and manicured and coifed receptionists. My concern is for procedures, processes, rules, norms, and incentives, implying changes in behaviour, forums for negotiation or exploration. The market, for example, is an institution. Many of these functions can be adopted by existing organizations. Nor is necessarily more coordination of functions involved. Some of these innovations can take a regional form (see below), others should be global.

11. The case for being utopian

Two types of objection can be made to the proposals of institutional reform: one on grounds of desirability, the other on grounds of feasibility. First, it may be said that creative institutions are not designed on a drawing board, but are the spontaneous responses to challenging situations. Designed institutions, such as the League of Nations, the World Economic Conference of 1933, the International Trade Charter, the Special Drawing Rights, all failed, while the multinational corporation, the Eurocurrency market, the globalisation of the 24-hour capital market and the swap arrangements between central banks, none of which sprang from grand designs, are considerable successes. The Bretton Woods institutions, which have served the world well for a quarter century, are the exception, but they were born after a world war and the complete breakdown of a previous order.

My reply would be that these spontaneous institutions themselves need designed institutions to regulate them. The debt crisis was a direct result of the unregulated recycling of OPEC surpluses by greedy lenders to profligate borrowers. Had something like an International Investment Trust that would have recycled the oil surpluses on acceptable terms to carefully selected projects and countries been in place in the seventies, we would have been spared many of the later pains. So much in reply to the charge that the proposals are undesirable.

A different criticism is that, though desirable, they are not feasible; they are utterly unrealistic and utopian. There are five replies to such criticisms, in defence of utopian proposals.

First, utopian thinking can be useful as a framework for analysis. Just as physicists assume an atmospheric vacuum for some purposes, so policy analysts can assume a political vacuum from which they can start afresh. The physicists' assumption plainly would not be useful for the design of parachutes, but can serve other purposes well. Similarly, when thinking of tomorrow's problems, utopianism is not helpful. But for long-term strategic purposes it is essential.

Second, the utopian vision gives a sense of direction, which can get lost in approaches that are preoccupied with the feasible. In a world that is regarded as the second-best of all feasible worlds, everything becomes a necessary constraint and all vision is lost.

Third, excessive concern with the feasible tends to reinforce the status quo. In negotiations, it strengthens the hand of those opposed to any reform. Unless the case for change can be represented in the same detail, it tends to be lost.

Fourth, it is sometimes the case that the conjuncture of circumstances changes quite suddenly and that the constellation of forces, unexpectedly, turns out to be favourable to even radical innovation. Unless we are prepared with a carefully worked out, detailed plan, that yesterday could have appeared utterly utopian, the reformers will lose out by default. Nobody expected the end of communism in Central and Eastern Europe, the disappearance of the Soviet Union, the fall of the Berlin Wall and the unification of Germany, the joining of NATO by Poland, Hungary and the Czech Republic, the break-up of Yugoslavia, the marketisation of China, the end of apartheid in South Africa, and the handshake on the White House lawn between the Israeli Prime Minister Yitzhak Rabin and the Palestinian leader Yasir Arafat.

Fifth, the utopian reformers themselves can constitute a pressure group, countervailing the self-interested pressures of the obstructionist groups. Ideas thought to be utopian have become realistic at moments in history when large numbers of people support them, and those in power have to yield to their demands. The demand for ending slavery is a historical example.

It is for these five reasons that utopians should not be discouraged from formulating their proposals and from thinking the unthinkable, unencumbered by the inhibitions and obstacles of political constraints, in the same detail that the defenders of the *status quo* devote to its elaboration and celebration. Utopianism and idealism will then turn out to be the most realistic vision.

There are three types of economist: those who can count and those who can't. But being able to count up to two, I want to distinguish between two types of people. Let us call them, for want of a better name, the Pedants and the Utopians.[75] The Pedants or technicians are those who know all the details about the way things are and work, that they have acquired an emotional vested interest in keeping them this way. I have come across them in the British civil service, in the bureaucracy of the World Bank, and elsewhere. They are admirable people but they are conservative, and not good companions for reform.

On the other hand there are the Utopians, the idealists, the visionaries who dare think the unthinkable. They are also admirable, many of them young people. But temperamentally they often lack the attention to detail that the Pedants have. When the day of the revolution comes, they will have entered it on the wrong date in their diaries and fail to turn up, or, if they do turn up, they will be on the wrong side of the barricades.

What we need is a marriage between the Pedants and the Utopians, between the realists who pay attention to the details and the idealists who have the vision of a better future. We need Pedantic Utopians or Utopian Pedants who will work out in considerable detail the ideal world and ways of getting to it, and promote the good causes with informed fantasy. Otherwise, when the opportunity arises, we shall miss it for lack of preparedness.

---

[75] The names are due to Peter Berger.

12. The role of micro-enterprises[76]

Globalisation refers not just to liberalisation and increase of trade in goods and services, but also to international movements of capital, technology, marketing and management. These in turn call for an understanding of the firm. Globalisation with its intensification of competition and expansion of the operations of multinational firms has sometimes hurt firms in the informal sector and micro-enterprises. It has put a premium on skills, size and power, and has penalised the low-skilled, small and weak. Many of these have disappeared as they were incapable of facing the competition, the size and the power of the large firms. On the other hand, there have been some positive effects, both direct and indirect, of globalisation on the informal sector. Exports have been encouraged, directly where there were institutions providing marketing, design and credit; and indirectly where the domestic formal sector subcontracted to informal enterprises.

There were some aspects of adjustment policies, liberalisation, privatisation, decentralisation and deregulation, normally regarded as hostile to the poor, that were favourable to the informal sector. Austerity programmes made some leaders more receptive to the needs of the poor. There was greater emphasis on jobs, incomes, the productivity of the poor. Even getting prices right can be used for the benefit of the informal sector. Kenya introduced a tariff rebate for small firms fifteen years after it was recommended in the Report of the ILO Commission. Balance of payments and debt problems, by restraining imports, can also favour the informal sector. The fashion for decentralisation can mean empowerment of poor groups with a switch to NGOs and against large state bureaucracies.

The relatively recent emphasis on the role of private enterprise and free markets has been useful. It has been partly a healthy reaction against excessive early faith in the power of governments to direct the economy, to manage businesses, and to correct market failures. But

---

[76] This section draws on Paul Streeten (1989 b) pp. 77-103.

unregulated markets can be both inefficient, and cruel. Joan Robinson said that the Invisible Hand can work by strangulation. We know that both markets and governments may fail, and that the failure of one does not automatically constitute a case for the other. It is now widely accepted that market failure is not necessarily a case for government intervention. It is less generally realized that government failure does not necessarily constitute a case for private enterprise and market forces. There is no *a priori* presumption as to which is preferable in any given situation.

The fact of government failure and bureaucratic failure suggests that it is important to concentrate the activities of the government on areas in which private efforts fail even more. Government activity often is complementary to private enterprise and efficient markets. The aim should be to avoid crowding out, and to achieve "crowding in." Government intervention should provide the conditions in which markets and enterprise can flourish. Market-orientation and state minimalism, far from going together, are incompatible. A well-designed policy calls for interventions to maintain competition and avoid restrictive practices, monopolies and cartels, to provide physical and social infrastructure and public goods, and some research efforts. It may also require new types of institutions. Governments should also take care of the victims of the competitive struggle, both for humanitarian and for efficiency reasons. The informal sector can play an important part in providing a safety net. But the policy of looking after these victims by encouraging the informal sector to provide a safety net (it should not be a safety hammock) can be carried out beyond this point and can make a substantial contribution to production and productivity growth.

The informal sector has been much discussed. It comprises four quite distinct groups. First, there are the self-employed, sometimes with unpaid members of their families. They are a heterogeneous group, ranging from shoeshine boys, street vendors, garbage collectors, petty thieves, prostitutes, drug traffickers, smugglers, and self-appointed tourist guides and bag carriers to jobbing gardeners, and small-scale producers such as blacksmiths, carpenters, sandal makers, lamp makers, bricklayers, bus and taxi drivers, seamstresses, repairmen, cobblers,   bakers,   shopkeepers,   auto   mechanics,   and builders who sometimes earn more than workers in the formal sector. Some formal sector workers use their savings to set up such enterprises for themselves in the informal sector.

Second, there are the casual workers, hired on a day-to-day basis in the docks, in construction, transport, and services. If the criterion for being in the informal sector is the method of hiring, then some workers hired casually by quite large firms should be counted as being in the informal sector.

Third, there are workers employed on a regular basis by small-scale, labour-intensive, not bureaucratically controlled firms outside the formal sector.

Fourth, there are the "outworkers," working in their homes under the putting-out system.

Another distinction is that between three quite different kinds of informal sector firm. First, there are the productive, entrepreneurial, often rapidly growing firms. They often graduate to middle-sized, and occasionally to large, firms. Secondly, there are the viable family firms, neither dynamic nor lame ducks that stand midway between the first and the third category. Third, there are the absorbers of the lame ducks thrown out of the formal sector, or incapable of entering it. Small family businesses of infirm, old or otherwise unemployable people. An elderly, infirm couple who live above their small grocery store, but are not bound by the laws about closing hours, might be entirely unemployable elsewhere. If their receipts exceed their costs, they earn a small producer's rent. They constitute the safety nets for personal incapacities and the disasters that befall people, and the shifts in demand or technology that occur in the formal sector.

The second type has been swollen in recent years by declining aggregate growth rates, austerity programmes and international competition that have thrown people out of employment in the formal sector. The activities of these firms are anti-cyclical, swelling with a decline in aggregate demand, and declining with its growth. At the same time, the crisis also provided opportunities for some firms who belong into the first category, although if they are linked, say through sub-contracting, to the formal sector, their behaviour will be pro-cyclical. Nevertheless, they benefit from fluctuations, for they will receive excess orders in booms, when the large firms run into capacity limits, and in slumps, when these firms wish to convert fixed into variable costs by hiving off employees and transforming them into subcontractors.

Informal sector firms, in the right setting, thrive on certain advantages over large-scale, formal sector firms. These advantages may be:

1. relating to location, when raw materials are dispersed and the enterprise processes them, or when markets are local and transport costs high;
2. relating to the process of production or the product, when the work requires simple assembly or other activities that are best carried out by hand or with simple tools;
3. relating to the market, when operating on a small scale for a local market has lower costs than larger-scale, more distant operation, or when the service has to be rendered where the customer is;
4. relating to adaptability and responsiveness to changing demand or technology, because of the absence of high fixed costs.

In the informal sector employment is largely supply-driven, absorbing fairly easily additional entrants (although there are also barriers to entry into some informal sector enterprises, particularly the need for some capital, and employment is offered by small businessmen *demanding* labour), whereas in the formal sector employment is largely demand-driven (although in the public sector there is a *supply*-driven component). There is also the enormous contribution of the work of women, until recently invisible in some cultures, who perform hard work without being counted as members of the labour force because their product is often not sold for cash.

According to the I.L.O. Kenya Report[77] informal sector activities are "a way of doing things, characterized by

---

[77] International Labour Office (1972) p. 6. Among other definitions of the informal sector are the following: self-employment; unpaid family workers, domestic servants and those self-employed who are not professionals and technicians; workers in small-scale units of production, sometimes including domestic servants and casual workers; sometimes also low-wage employees of 'modern' firms; unprotected, unregulated economic activities; illegal, clandestine and unregistered activities; 'traditional' sector; 'subsistence' sector; 'marginalized mass'; very small economic units or micro-businesses; an abnormally swollen, overdistended tertiary sector of minimal productivity; a sector in which wage rates equal marginal productivity. For sources of these and other definitions, see Michael Hopkins (1989) pp. 69-73.

a. ease of entry;
b. reliance on indigenous resources;
c. family ownership of enterprises;
d. small scale operations;
e. labour-intensive and adapted technology;
f. skills acquired outside the formal educational system;
g. unregulated and competitive markets."

It is easy to dismiss the informal sector as a useless concept.[78] It is equally easy to romanticize it and to think of it as a potential of high productivity, of competitive capitalism, harassed and discriminated against by mercantilistic, predatory and interfering bureaucrats.

The informal sector certainly is a very heterogeneous collection of people, activities and firms. There are some whose marginal productivity is zero or negative, because their activities only take away from the sales of others, or because they only create nuisances and then extract payment for their removal. Beggars, petty thieves, small vendors, providers of unwanted and forced services are manifestations of disguised unemployment. Even genuinely productive firms often break the law and evade taxes. Many informal sector employers exploit their workers at least as much as formal sector employers. There is no point in glamourizing them, or in overstating their contribution to production.

Another way in which the informal sector has been misleadingly romanticized is by holding it up as a splendid example of entrepreneurial competition and free enterprise capitalism. The informal sector has its peculiar modes of behaviour and formalities. As the studies of Hernando de Soto (one of the leading proponents of this form of activity) and of Judith Tendler have shown, relations between firms in the informal sector are sometimes characterized by a striking degree of cooperation.[79]

---

[78] For a well reasoned criticism of the concept see Lisa Peattie (1987) pp. 851-860. Although the critique by L. Peattie is well argued, I do not think it necessarily leads to the abandonment of the concept. The exploration of the specific linkages, some positive, others negative, between firms and policies that she asks for can surely be done within the conceptual framework suggested by the 'informal sector'.

[79] See Hernando de Soto (1987).

They share inputs when these are in scarce supply; when one firm has a large contract and its neighbour does not, it shares the contract with the other firm by subcontracting or hiring its owner as a temporary worker; there is work-sharing not only among firms, but also when the demand for labour is reduced. Not much attention has been paid to this fact, partly because it contradicts the idealized individualistic picture of firms in active competition.[80]

While, on the one hand, the informal sector should not be idealized, there are, on the other hand, actually or potentially highly productive small enterprises, some of whose owners earn more than some workers in the formal sector. They tend to use more labour per unit of capital and per unit of output, and often use it intensively, remuneratively, and highly efficiently.[81]

In Peru some informal sector firms absorb those who wish to, but cannot, enter the formal sector. In Argentina, on the other hand, people with secure but ill-paid jobs in the formal sector opt to earn extra income and gain additional mobility in the informal sector.

Some people who work in the informal sector also work in the formal sector. Occasionally members of the same family are engaged in both. Some characteristics of the informal sector can be found in the formal sector, such as casual hiring of labour. Some firms are informal with respect to some of their activities (not paying certain taxes, working without some licences, casually hiring some of their workers), and formal with respect to others. We have seen that some informal sector incomes are higher than some formal sector earnings. It is impossible to count and record the informal sector, because, by its nature, no official records exist.[82] But in spite of these obstacles to a clear and neat definition, the concept meets a real need.

---

[80] See Judith Tendler (1987).

[81] Some caution is necessary. Obviously, not all small-scale, informal sector enterprises are efficient, or economize even in the use of capital. The working capital requirements of small enterprises are often higher than those of larger ones. And even the lower capital/labour ratio can be bought at the cost of a higher capital/output ratio. But the scheme proposed below should ensure that such waste is minimized. For evidence of the efficiency of small-scale industries (overlapping with the informal sector, though not identical), see Carl Liedholm and Donald Mead (1997).

[82] Since less interventionist governments will tend to include in their national accounts activities that more interventionist governments do not count, because they are illegal, it is easy to overstate the growth performance of countries that have followed the World Bank's advice to rely more on markets. World Bank reports have not always paid attention to this distortion of growth figures in comparing good and poor performers.

There are those who believe that the informal sector is entirely the creature of mistaken government policies. "Get the prices right, deregulate, decentralize, liberalize and privatize, and the informal sector will disappear." The evidence does not show, however, that modern technology, even with the most "realistic" equilibrium prices for labour, capital and foreign exchange, can absorb the numbers of workers who will be seeking jobs at wages that can support them.

There are four reasons for paying attention to the informal sector. They arise from the triple needs to increase production, employment (a source of recognition and self-respect), and incomes, and the need to avoid rebellion.

First, the informal sector represents a potentially large reserve of productivity and earning power. Although not all informal sector activities contribute actually or potentially to productivity and earnings, some do.

Secondly, the labour force in the low-income countries is likely to grow rapidly in the next fifteen years and neither agriculture nor the industrial formal sector is capable of absorbing even a fraction of these additions, to say nothing of the large number of already unemployed or underemployed. The International Labor Organization issued a report in January 2001 that said that 500 million new jobs will be needed over the next ten years in order to employ new arrivals in the job market and reduce existing global unemployment by half. The majority of these new job seekers, approximately two thirds, will be Asians. In sub-Saharan Africa workers seeking remunerative employment had been estimated to grow at a rate of 2-3 per cent per year. It was once thought that the labour-surplus economies of Java and Bangladesh represented the future for Africa. This has to be revised in the light of the terrible HIV/AIDS crisis. According to a recent United Nations report about half of all 15-year olds in the African countries worst affected by AIDS will die of the disease, even if rates of infection drop substantially. If infection rates remain high, more than two-thirds of the 15-year-old will die from AIDS. The impact of HIV/AIDS in sub-Saharan will be a greatly reduced labour force, especially among skilled and professional workers. There will be a rise in child labour, especially of orphans whose parents have died or are incapacitated by AIDS. The general job situation is further aggravated by the low world economic growth rates. The combination of globalisation, population growth, urbanization and recession has swelled the informal sector, which presents the only hope for jobs.[83]

A third reason for paying attention to the informal sector is that, although the informal sector should not be equated with the poor (we have seen that some members of the informal sector earn more than some in the formal sector and many poor are outside the informal sector), it is in the informal sector where many poor people are to be found. By harnessing its potential for generating incomes (and self-respect), not only efficient growth is promoted but also poverty is reduced. If its productivity and remunerativeness can be raised without depriving the high-productivity sector of resources, and hence not only of more production but also of the opportunity of future employment, there is no conflict between efficiency and equity.

A fourth reason is that prolonged unemployment leads to alienation and a sense of worthlessness, and can be a source of rebellious instead of productive activity. Particularly governments in power have an interest in stability, in not upsetting the existing order, and in using the informal sector as a vote bank.

Normally one would wish the informal sector neither to be subsidized at the expense of the high-productivity formal sector firms, nor to be squeezed out by the privileged treatment of formal sector firms.

The task then is to make these informal sector enterprises complementary to the larger-scale, formal sector firms, including foreign multinational corporations and foreign importing firms. Now they are often competitive, and, aided by the government, the large firms often drive out the small ones. Both Mao's declared strategy of walking on two legs and the success of the Japanese in combining a modern and a small-scale industrial sector illustrate the possibility of successfully combining the two. The East Asian success stories

---

[83] This approach has been criticized as excessively Eurocentric. The critics say, the notion of a "labour force" comprising all able-bodied men and women between, say fifteen and sixty, is not applicable to many developing countries. The problem is not to find jobs, but to redefine "work". The "idleness" of the women in purdah, the gossips in the cafés, the begging priests and monks, the small-scale rentiers, the useless peddlers, the idle bureaucrats, should, according to Clifford Geertz, not be suppressed and these people should not be encouraged to "work", but the notions of "idleness" and "work" should be redefined, so that these "underemployed" are kept "outside the work force but inside society." See Clifford Geertz (1969) pp. 34-34. The evidence does not seem to have confirmed that this is the preference of the workless, whenever opportunities to earn arise. It would, however, be worth exploring whether activities in the informal sector that do not show high economic returns may not be valuable by some other standards.

illustrate how foreign firms can undertake the marketing of manufactured exports. In Singapore, it was transnational corporations that marketed the output of wholly or majority-owned local subsidiaries. In other countries it was the importers in the advanced countries, retail and department stores, wholesalers or trading companies, that performed these functions. The Koreans used foreign buyers in the early stages of development not only to sell their goods but also to acquire knowledge about styles, designs, and technologies. The current trend towards modular manufacturing and sourcing, and just-in-time methods of production, according to which some quite small firms produce components for assembly in large firms, also encourages the growth of informal sector firms. All these are illustrations of ways of using the power of the large firms, the Goliaths, in their self-interest, for the benefit of the poor, the little Davids, rather as a judo fighter uses the power of his opponent for his purposes. Let us call this the judo trick, partly because it uses the leverage of an initially antagonistic force with multiplied effect, and partly because it uses the force of what is usually regarded as a powerful, strong opponent for the benefit of the weak. In this way small enterprises that would otherwise either never come into existence or would die can grow and flourish.

One model for such a symbiosis in agriculture has been pioneered by the British Commonwealth Development Corporation first in the Kulai oil palm project in Malaysia and then in the Kenya Tea Development Authority and other projects. A modern nucleus estate does the management, the processing, the exporting, the marketing, and provides the extension services and the credit for a group of smallholders clustered round the estate. The activities best carried out on a large scale, with modern techniques, are done by the nucleus estate, while the growing of the crop is done by newly settled smallholders. This type of project has proved highly successful, although as done by the Commonwealth Development Corporation it is rather management-intensive and the calls on skilled professional management and extension services would have to be reduced if it were to be replicated on a large scale in labour surplus economies, such as those of South Asia. Another model is the National Dairy Development Board in India. The production of milk, largely by women, remains traditional and informal, while processing, credit and marketing follow modern, formal sector lines.

A similar model has been followed by private foreign agro-businesses. It has been called the "core-satellite" model, or contract farming or smallholder outgrower scheme.[84] Companies like Heinz, Del Monte, United Brands, Nestlé and Shell, provide marketing, equipment, technical assistance, credit, fertilizer, and other inputs, as well as ancillary services, and smallholders grow fruit and vegetables. In order to balance bargaining power in drawing up contracts, the smallholders have to be organized. Then they can use their power both directly and indirectly on the government to give them political support. The high fixed costs of processing plant make it important for the company to secure an even and certain flow of inputs, which is ensured by the contract. It is preferable to either open market purchases or a plantation with hired labour, though contract farming is sometimes supplemented by these other forms. The smallholders, in turn, acquire an assured market, credit and inputs at low costs. I do not advocate the replication of these schemes, for too little research has been done on the precise division of gains and conditions for the optimum smallholder benefit, but these are worth exploring.

This type of institutional arrangement can combine some of the advantages of plantation farming, such as quality control, coordination of interdependent stages of production and marketing, with those of smallholder production, such as autonomy, keener incentives and income generation for poor people. But the possibility of abuse of its monopsonistic power by the private company against the smallholders makes it necessary to have either smallholder organizations with countervailing power or independent public regulation.

No similar type of institutional arrangement exists as yet in manufacturing. One can easily imagine a large, modern manufacturing plant round which are clustered informal, small, enterprises doing repairs, manufacturing components and spare parts, and providing ancillary services such as transport, handling, cleaning, packaging, catering, etc. The nearest thing to such an arrangement is the system of modular manufacturing. It has, for example, replaced or perhaps complemented the assembly line as a method of manufacturing cars. It involves designing and assembling an entire motor car as a series of sub-assemblies, or modules. Suppliers of these components (e.g.

---

[84] David J. Glover (1984) pp. 1143-1157 and (1987) pp. 441-448. Also Arthur Goldsmith (1985) pp. 1125-138 and the Special Issue on Contract Farming and Smallholder Outgrower Schemes in Eastern and Southern Africa of the *East Africa Economic Review* (1989).

dashboards, sunroofs or doors), with their lower labour costs, could concentrate on the nuts and bolts, leaving to the large firms styling, packaging, marketing and distribution. Another approximation is the Japanese *kanban* system with the little sub-contractors, often retired ex-employees of the firm, clustered round the large firm.

Such a project, to make use of informal sector enterprises, would require changes in government policies. The first step would be to stop repressive regulation, harassment and discrimination against the informal sector; to stop, for example, demolishing informal sector houses, subject, of course, to some urban planning for open spaces. In Peru a Union of Formals and Informals has been formed to reduce government regulations and bureaucratic meddling.[85] It is an interesting example of a reformist alliance, in which formal sector enterprises make common cause with informal ones, sharing with them their experience and uniting in exercising political pressure. The next step would be to adopt policies and to create institutions with respect to the provision of credit, training, information and imported inputs (e.g. tariff remission for the informal sector). As to credit, innovative steps are needed for small loans and new types of collateral, such as inventories, or an unlicensed bus, or plots of land in shantytowns. Another option is the mobilization of peer pressure, as in the Grameen Bank in Bangladesh. A third step would be to remove legislation that gives the formal sector special advantages in buying from or selling to the informal sector.

The implications of this proposal for policy are quite radical. For example, the common prescription is to lower real wages in the formal sector in order to raise employment. But in this model, a rise in real wages may increase employment and incomes in the informal sector.

---

[85] See "Peruvians Combating Red Tape" by Alan Riding (1988) p. 3. This article cites Hernando de Soto, head of the Institute for Liberty and Democracy in Lima, that 60 per cent of Peru's work force operates outside the formal economy and accounts for 38 per cent of its gross domestic product. 95 per cent of public transport in Lima is in the hands of informal operators, 98 per cent of new homes, most of them in shantytowns, are built without permits, and 80 cent of clothing, and 60 per cent of furniture are produced by the informal sector. According to the same source it takes 289 days to register a new company, so most people do not bother. See also Hernando de Soto (1989). The book contains an impassioned introduction by Mario Vargas Llosa. There de Soto estimates that in Peru the informal sector makes up 48% of the total labour force. Its members work 61% of all man-hours and create 38% of the GDP. They have set up 274 markets in Lima; they run 93% of the buses; and they have built 42% of the houses. See also "An Interview with Hernando de Soto" in *Health and Development* (1989). There are, however critics of de Soto's enthusiasm. Jaime Mezzera, with the International Labour Organisation (PREALC) in Santiago, estimates the informal sector's contribution in any Latin American country at no more than 15 per cent.

The production of spare parts, repairs, and ancillary activities, such as cleaning, transport, packaging, are carried out inside the firms in the organized sector while wages are low. When they are raised, these activities become worth contracting out to small informal sector firms not subject to minimum wage legislation. These firms carry out these activities in a more labour-intensive way, and benefit from the new contracts. Even if the workers previously engaged on these activities inside the formal sector firms were to be dismissed (rather than redeployed), and were to add pressure on incomes in the informal sector, the savings in capital and profits may be enough to produce higher incomes as well as more jobs for the sub-contractors. This would be the case, for example, if the self-employed small entrepreneur works harder than the same man as paid foreman or manager. A similar effect is produced by legislating for a shorter working week, to which the informal sector firms are not bound. Higher taxes, avoided or evaded by these enterprises, work in the same direction.[86]

It is true that, for such efficient and income-raising sub-contracting to occur, the initial in-house production by the formal firms may have been sub-optimal. For, it may be argued, if it pays to sub-contract at the higher wage, it would have done so also at the lower wage. In this case stubbornness, inertia or ignorance stood in the way, and the rise in the wage alerts the businessman. But there may have been non-pecuniary offsetting advantages in in-house production, which are more than offset when costs rise. These may be the result of transport, communication or transaction costs, or high training costs with greater probability that the trained subcontractor may leave than the in-house worker.

Other linkages between formal and informal sector firms affecting competing and complementary inputs and products should be carefully traced.[87] If high and modern growth rates in the formal sector are not to be impeded, it is important not to deprive it of scarce factors, such as capital, management or wage goods, in order to benefit low productivity activities. This implies that the capital and organizational

---

[86] Ronald Dore has suggested that the same effect can be achieved by the Japanese practice of high average wages with lifetime employment and a retirement age at 50. The worker then sets himself up in a small subcontracting business, and makes use of his connection with the large firm, which regards him as loyal and reliable.

[87] Sanjaya Lall distinguishes between the following linkages. Establishment, locational, informational, technical, financial, raw material procurement, managerial, pricing, other distributional, and diversificationp. See Sanjaya Lall (1985) pp. 269-270.

capacity should be recruited from within the informal sector. At the same time, it is also important that the expansion of the formal sector should not raise the prices of goods necessary for production in the informal sector. This appears to have happened in Colombia, where a housing project for the rich was intended to generate incomes for workers. But the resulting price increase in concrete and steel led to price rises in sheet metal and cardboard, jeopardizing the building efforts of the poor.[88]

Another illustration is to be found in a modern version of the 18th century putting-out system. Subcontracting by large firms to small, sometimes informal sector firms or cottage industries, is quite common in the developing world. But there is still much scope for importing houses in advanced countries or retail chains independent of developed country producer interests to apply the putting-out system to informal sector firms in developing countries. The large firm provides the materials, the designs, the credit and the marketing, while the informal sector firm produces the clothes, the sport equipment, the electronic components, the cloth and woodwork for handicrafts, or the crops. The British retail chain Marks and Spencer have employed this modern putting-out system not only in England but also in some developing countries. Coats Viyella, a British clothing company, has run a factory in Mauritius since 1992. Workers there cut, stitch and pack each week 36,000 cotton shirts for Marks and Spencer. The firm has had to search abroad for workers, even recruiting 130 machinists, mostly women, from China.

There opens up another use for the judo trick. The political power of these retail chains, independent of domestic producer interests, such as Atlantic and Pacific Stores or Safeways, can be used to counteract the pressures for protection of the producer lobbies in the developed countries. Their interest in low-cost, labour-intensive imports coincides with those of the poor producers in the developing countries. If institutional safeguards are adopted to prevent exploitation and sweated labour, firms such as Marks and Spencer can do more for the poor of the world than Marx and Engels.

---

[88] See Lisa Peattie (1987) p. 858. The terms of trade between the informal and formal sectors are an important determinant of the division of gains. The "reserve army of unemployed" will tend to keep incomes and prices of informal firms low, while productivity growth in formal firms will tend to be passed on in higher wages, rather than lower prices. In addition, there may be unequal bargaining power. An "unequal exchange" may result.

In addition to new institutions, policies will have to be revised. Thus, many economists have opposed minimum wage legislation on the ground that it prevents higher employment. But, as we have seen, if a higher wage level or a shorter working week, applied only to organized sector firms, forces them to contract out to the informal sector activities previously carried out inside these firms, this can be a gain in employment and earnings. For these activities are likely to be carried out in a more labour-intensive way in the informal sector than they were inside the large firms. One characteristic of the distinction is the flexibility of incomes in the informal sector compared with rigidity downwards in the formal sector. Therefore its absorptive capacity of labour is higher and policies that make it worth while to give more business to the small firms are to be welcomed.

The measures needed to implement such a policy can be summarized under the following headings:

1. First, a more favourable economic environment for the informal sector should be created. At present, macropolicies tend to discriminate against it. For example, investment incentives confine tax concessions to formal sector firms. Overvaluation of the exchange rate combined with import restrictions and undervaluation of the interest rate handicap the access to inputs and credit of informal firms.

2. Second, it is necessary to design new institutions of the kind indicated above. The access of the poor to assets should be improved. In agriculture this policy has worked. It is more difficult to apply it in urban industry. Steps are being taken to provide these small entrepreneurs with credit. The Grameen Bank in Bangladesh has found many imitators in other countries. The Inter-American Development Bank wants to establish itself as the bank for Latin America's informal sector. The International Fund for Agricultural Development has successfully lent to businesses without collateral. Pressures for repayment can be exercised by peer groups, and by making small loans for short periods. Loans should be primarily for working capital. Judgment of the borrower's reliability can replace conventional collateral requirements.

3. Third, returns to these enterprises must be raised. It is not enough, as is often said, to raise their productivity, for productivity gains can be passed on in the form of lower prices to often better off buyers in the formal sector, or offset by charging higher prices for inputs. It is

the earning power, the remunerativeness of the enterprise that matters.

4. Fourth, employment opportunities must be improved. Even though the informal sector is often defined as supply-driven, there are obstacles to entry and to employment, which should be reduced.

5. Fifth, the demand for their production should be raised. Since poor people tend to buy the goods produced by the poor people in the informal sector, policies that generate incomes by poor people will also raise the demand for their products.[89]

6. Sixth, access to education, training and health services must be improved, both as an end in itself and in order to raise the productivity of the poor. Technical training and instruction in simple managerial techniques, such as cost accounting and book keeping, marketing and technical know-how are important. The identification and provision of missing components, such as market information, infrastructure or technical know-how can yield great benefits at little cost.

7. Seventh, transfer payments out of public funds are also required to provide a safety net, not only for the unemployables, the disabled, the sick, the old, but also to tide people over periods of no earnings, of failure of their enterprises or temporary inability to work.

It is customary to distinguish between primary incomes, earned through production and sales for the market; secondary incomes resulting from access to the sources of improved earning power, such as education, training and health services; and tertiary incomes which are pure welfare payments. The unemployables would receive tertiary incomes. Even these, while not raising productivity, may lower reproductivity. The need to be looked after in old age or in case of an accident is one of the reasons for the desire for many children, particularly sons. If the community looks after the disabled, infirm and old, an important motive for a large family disappears.

Another way of categorizing the necessary public sector measures to make the symbiosis between multinational corporations and the informal sector successful can be summarized with a mnemotechnic device. It is the seven 'Ins' or *In*struments:

---

[89] See Liedholm and Mead (1987) and Radha Sinha, Peter Pearson, Gopal Kadekodi and Mary Gregory (1979).

1. Incentives: prices of both inputs and outputs must be right.
2. Inputs: both imported and domestic inputs, including credit, must be available.
3. Institutions: access to marketing institutions and credit institutions and a non-corrupt, efficient administrative apparatus must exist.
4. Innovation: the right small-scale technology, appropriate for small enterprises often does not exist and research and search should be provided to create or find, and adapt it.
5. Information: a knowledge bank for technology should provide means of spreading the results of research and search among the firms. Also instruction in management, bookkeeping, and recording should be provided.
6. Infrastructure: roads, communications, harbours, and utilities must be available if the output of the informal sector is to be sold in national and international markets.
7. Independence and Initiative: permit and encourage self-reliance and liberate people from excessive regulation and harassment.

We might add to this Inconsistency, which can be a virtue in a largely unknown situation in which trial and error and learning by mistakes are the best ways to proceed.

In the manner described above, the informal sector can be made complementary to the formal sector and linked with the global economy, with respect to access to markets, inputs, information and technology, the small-scale firms to large-scale firms, domestic to foreign firms, public to private firms, and non-governmental organizations to governments. The putting-out system of foreign retailers or importing houses is an example of the symbiosis between foreign large and domestic small enterprises. Similarly, private voluntary organizations engaged in helping informal sector projects should find ways of cooperating with government departments and multinational corporations, which are often in a better position to finance and replicate successful projects.

Our knowledge of the informal sector in most developing countries is still rudimentary. What we need is both time series and cross-country studies of informal sector activities to show at what income levels, with what policies, which activities, actually or potentially, contribute to employment, productivity, earning power, production, and growth.

It has already been emphasized that the encouragement of complementarities should not be done at the expense of the growth of the high-productivity, modern sector. On the contrary, the small units should contribute to raising the productivity of the large ones. According to S. P. Kashyap, handicaps for large firms and biases in policy against them are largely responsible for the growth of small-scale enterprises in India.[90] Nor should there be any form of exploitation, such as child labour, inhuman working conditions, sweated labour, or monopsonistic depression of the prices at which outputs are bought. Fears have been expressed that the informal sector enterprises have been reduced to a state of "peonage" by their formal sector principals.[91] Nor should there be monopolistic overpricing of the intermediate products supplied by the formal sector as inputs to the informal enterprises. Such overpricing could be the result of import restrictions or other barriers to entry. In Sierra Leone the large-scale flour mill, which supplies flour to small-scale bakers, is protected by an exclusive import licence, and therefore can sell its flour at prices over twice those of potential imports.[92] The policies must be designed to mobilize the energies of the small-scale firms, and to make use of their lower costs, more labour-intensive techniques, greater employment creation, and wider dispersion of technology, without, on the one hand, sacrificing efficiency and innovation, and, on the other, depriving the informal sector, by underpricing outputs or overpricing inputs, of adequate rewards and humane working conditions.

Encouragement that the informal sector, or at any rate the sector containing small-scale firms, can be the dynamic sector of the future comes from an unexpected source: the literature on Flexible Specialization, mainly applied to trends in the advanced, industrial countries.[93] The move from standardized, large-scale mass production to small-scale, flexible firms is the result of changes in demand and in supply. On the demand side, the mass consumer has been replaced by a more sophisticated type with higher purchasing power and more differentiated tastes. On the side of supply, the technology for energy and information has encouraged decentralization of production and smaller size of firms. "Mass production is the manufacture of standard

---

[90] S.P. Kashyap (1988) pp. 67-681.
[91] Sanjaya Lall (1985) p. 270. Lall, however, concludes from his case study that "on the whole, their benefits from being linked outweigh their costs" p. 288.
[92] Enyinna Chuta and Carl Liedholm (1985) p. 144.
[93] See Judith Tendler (1987) and Charles F. Sabel (1987) pp. 27-55.

products with specialized resources...; flexible specialization is the production of specialized products with general resources..."[94] In Mexico the large number of small, decentralized workshops (maquilas) and household units are subcontractors for the large firms. The uncertainties of the 1980s have encouraged the rise of these units that produce specialized products with a broadly skilled and weakly specialized labour force. The division of labour resembles the Japanese *kanban* where many small suppliers and subcontractors are clustered round a large firm. Similar patterns are to be found in Northern Italy (the so-called "Third Italy") and other parts of Europe, with their regional clusters of small, cooperating, flexible firms.[95] As demand and technology change, skills and products can be easily switched and adapted to the new situation. The shoe industries around Novo Hamburgo in Brazil and Leòn in Mexico are organized on this basis and have encouraged the growth of rural industries. As Judith Tendler has pointed out, there has been a role reversal, and in this literature the formal sector firms, interpreted as the traditional, large-scale, fixed-cost, mass-production firms, are seen as "sick," whereas the flexible, small firms are capable of responding dynamically to changing demand and technology. Not only have they taken over the function of leadership, but they are also more humane and responsible in their work relations. There is also a new form of cooperation between the small firms, and the old confrontation between labour and capital is replaced by one between the managers, owners and workers in the small, subcontracting firms, on the one hand, and the large buyers of their output on the other. In addition, supportive local institutions evolve that provide information, technical know-how and training. One does not have to accept the view of the disappearance of the large firm to accept the growing role of these small enterprises. Indeed, the thesis propounded here is that the two should become complementary. All this holds out great productive and social promise for the informal sector, especially if supported by the right social policies.

---

[94] See Charles F. Sabel (1987) p. 40. The *marxisant* terms are "Fordism" and "post-Fordism," not, of course named after the Ford Foundation but after Henry Ford and his famous remark that the American public could have their model T any colour they liked as long as it was black.

[95] Recent evidence shows, however, that some of these firms in the Third Italy have gone bankrupt, others have been taken over by large firms. It seems that they have a tendency to merge either into the first or into the second Italy.

13. Global financial flows

Global financial flows have enormously increased and now are on an average day about $ 1.5 trillion. 40 per cent of these transactions are reversed within two days and 80 per cent within seven days. This represents a ratio of foreign exchange dealings to world trade of nearly 70:1 and equals the world's total official gold and foreign exchange reserves. In 1971 about 90 per cent of all foreign exchange transactions were for the finance of trade and long-term investment, and only 10 per cent were speculative. Today, these percentages are reversed; well over 90 per cent of all transactions are speculative.[96] The enormous growth of these flows is the result of the collapse of the Bretton Woods system of fixed exchange rates in 1973 combined with deregulation and liberalisation of capital flows, and the opportunities this has provided for speculation on variable exchange rates.

The 24-hour international capital market has given rise to the fear that the international financial system is unstable. A run on any one country's currency can easily spread to other countries and lead to a collapse of values on stock exchanges, of markets and of whole economies. It has been argued that recent difficulties point to the strength, rather than the weakness, of the international system. The effects of the different crises - the Latin American debt crisis, the American savings-and-loan fiasco, the BCCI scandal, Mexico, Barings, Daiwa, the 1997/99 crisis in Asia and Brazil - did not spread internationally. Many individuals were hurt, including tax-payers, but these were mainly residents in the area and the rest of the world was sheltered. The system did not break down - at least so far. Obviously, this does not mean that it cannot do so in future. The summer of 1998 came near to such a breakdown. The precariousness of the world economy is plain and steps towards a substantial strengthening of the IMF or, better, a global central bank should be taken. As lender of last resort and creator of new money it would have to be able to lend freely,

---

[96] John Eatwell (1995) p. 277.

with much larger resources than are now at the disposal of the IMF, at penal interest rates, and against collateral. It would reduce the debts of some developing countries and oversee the operations of shaky financial institutions. It would buy the debt of a country in difficulties and perhaps later resell it at a profit. It would be accountable to an enlarged Group of 7, with additional membership rotating between countries like Mexico, Brazil, South Africa, Poland, India, China and South Korea. The absence of institutions such as a central bank, a Securities and Exchange Commission, the insurance of bank deposits, or safety nets at the global level, while free markets run wild, accounts for the global turmoil in the stock markets of the world. The problem with creating such an institution is that of the leaky roof that never gets repaired. When the sun shines, there is no need, and when it rains, nobody wants to get wet. When all goes well, nobody is interested in creating such an institution, and in a crisis, officials are preoccupied with grappling with it.

The stunning increase in long-term private foreign investment has built roads, airports and factories in developing countries. Private flows to developing countries have increased from $ 34 billion in 1987 to $ 256 billion in 1997. They have brought much needed capital to these countries and good returns to the investors. But large inflows can be reversed and become large outflows, as Mexico in 1994-1995 and the Asian financial crisis in 1997-1998 have shown. Moreover, capital mobility in the presence of trade distortions results in a misallocation of capital and a deterioration of the well-being of people in the capital-importing countries. If capital flows freely into a labour-rich country that protects its capital-intensive industries (such as steel and car production), capital will be misallocated, the country's national product at world prices will be reduced and its national income will be reduced further by the payment of returns to the foreign capital. Countries that impose rules and regulations restricting the purchase and sale of currencies, such as China and Chile, have fared best in times of crisis. (Chile, however, has eliminated some of these controls in 1998.)

Globalisation of financial and real flows, as of trade, has been partial; there are hardly any flows to low-income countries; and while private flows to middle-income developing countries have enormously increased, official development assistance has stagnated. The bulk of the flows is between OECD countries; and there is some foreign investment in a selected group of developing countries, mostly in Latin America, East Asia and China. According to the World Bank, 95 per cent of private flows to developing countries in 1996 went to just 26 countries; 140 countries shared the remaining 5 per cent. And these private flows are highly volatile, tending to be withdrawn at short notice. The intra-OECD flows contradict neoclassical theory, according to which capital should flow from the capital-abundant to the capital-scarce countries. In fact, the USA, one of the capital-richest countries, has attracted most capital, in 1996/97 over $ 160 billion per year. And among developing countries it is those with substantial human capital and good government policies that attract financial capital.

Some pessimists have two contradictory worries: first, that a massive outflow of capital from rich to poor countries will exports jobs; second, that cheap imports from the South will lead to a current account deficit of the North (which must mean a capital flow from the South to the North) and therefore again to job losses. Neither should be a cause for worry in the long run. A current account deficit of the South is more likely when the Asian crisis has passed, and the resulting expanding markets in the South will create jobs in the North, although these will be different from current ones and this means reeducation and redeployment of labour.

In the light of this large increase in financial flows, it is a puzzle to find that domestic savings and investment are closer together for most countries than they were before 1914. It follows that net flows are much smaller than gross flows. As we have seen, many explanations have been offered for this paradox, among them the possible obstacle to long-term real investment and consequential global integration of fluctuating exchange rates. Deregulation and liberalisation have accelerated neither investment nor growth, nor resulted in high levels of employment nor in a better income distribution, nor in lower borrowing costs. They have also increased the volatility of asset prices.

Global financial deregulation and liberalisation have brought some benefits but also greater risks for investors and the financial system. In the 1980s the task of stabilising against high inflation, the debt crisis and structural adjustment preoccupied many governments. In the 1990s problems of coping with rapid swings in capital flows had become more pressing, highlighted by Mexico's financial crisis in 1995 and the troubles in South Korea, Thailand, Malaysia, Indonesia and the Philippines in 1997/98. Suddenly government was called upon to bail out the financiers who previously had preached the virtues of free markets. The cause of the East Asian financial crisis, as Robert Wade has said, "was a structure of financial claims that involved too much short-term debt relative to long-term debt, too much debt relative to equity, too much foreign debt relative to total debt, too much foreign equity relative to domestic equity."[97] This raised the question whether a return to control of capital markets is indicated. In developing countries regulations that favour direct foreign investment over purchases of shares, that inhibit short-term flows, and that discourage local firms from accumulating large foreign debts are again being discussed.

There is a need for re-regulation and harmonisation of legislation. The more free-enterprise-oriented a country is, the greater the need for official supervision. Deregulation has resulted in higher and less stable interest rates, less stable exchange rates, boom and slump in property prices, gambling on asset values, interest and exchange rates. Excessive deregulation, allowing firms to borrow abroad without any government control or coordination, has led to the run on the currencies. The danger of business and bank failures is high. If we wish not to have to bail out financial institutions, deregulation has to be supported by close and well-coordinated supervision.

The Bretton Woods system was based on the premise that currency convertibility, multilateral trade and stable exchange rates require constraints on international capital mobility. Financial liberalisation, carried too far, can damage the more important trade liberalisation. For example, when a country should devalue because its prices have risen by more than foreign prices, it may be unable to do so because of speculative short-term capital inflows. Or changes in capital flows can produce large swings in the exchange rate, which are detrimental to trade. One way to slow down short-term capital movements would be the Tobin tax, a small, uniform tax imposed on all international capital flows. There has been a good deal of recent discussion, and a book has been published that discusses the desirability and feasibility of the tax, both for and against it.[98] More ambitiously, a new global institution has been proposed that would supervise the participants in the global capital market and establish trading, reporting and disclosure requirements.

---

[97] Robert Wade (1999).
[98] Mahbub ul Haq, Inge Kaul and Isabelle Grunberg (editors) (1996).

14. International migration and brain drain

The tripod of globalisation comprises liberalisation of trade in goods and services, in capital flows (or free trade in assets), and free movement of people. Policies of the industrial countries have, with some interruptions, embraced in principle the first two, but have not extended to the third. But there are strong arguments that the advanced industrial countries should be more open to immigration than they are, even if only in their own national self-interest and disregarding ethical and humanitarian arguments. The reasons for this are primarily though not exclusively economic. Immigrant groups have caused unrest and disorder, and complaints about destroying cultural identity, but cultural diversity can also enrich a society and immigrants often display desirable cultural characteristics such as the work ethic, individual responsibility, concern for the family, etc. to a greater extent than the native population. Immigrants are likely to be young people of working age, with good qualifications and motivations; they will tend to save more, work harder, and start new businesses; they are likely to contribute more through taxes than they receive from public revenue, and there is no reason to believe that they would increase unemployment, though unemployment would be more likely to be avoided if the increase in immigration were to be spread over a long period.[99]

More recent research in the USA has challenged some of these conclusions. It has shown that one must distinguish between different groups of immigrants. If the contribution of immigrants is measured by the wage gap between them and native-born Americans, Latin American immigrants earn less, and the wage gap has actually widened. Although low wages of immigrants have benefits to

---

[99] For a fuller treatment see David Henderson (1993) and Julian L. Simon (1989). Simon argues that the positive effects are likely to outweigh what he calls the dilusion of capital.

consumers of the goods they produce, these immigrants are more likely to become a burden on the social services.[100]

A common view both in the USA and in Europe is that the promotion of development in the developing countries by the rich countries through development aid, technical assistance, private investment and trade would reduce the pressure of migration. If people can find remunerative jobs in their own countries they will not want to emigrate. The two legs of the tripod are sufficient - so the argument goes - to make the third unnecessary.

But there is another side to this. One has to distinguish between the incentives to migrate and the means to migrate. Incentives may be somewhat reduced, but they will remain as long as earnings differentials remain as high as they are likely to be in the foreseeable future. Factor price equalisation is not likely to occur soon. But industrialisation and development means restructuring, which in turn means loss of jobs, which would restore the incentive to emigrate. The means to migrate would, of course, increase as local opportunities and incomes improve and as travel costs drop. Mexican and Central American immigrants would no longer have to swim across the Rio Grande but would be able to afford a boat, and migrants into Europe instead of walking could drive across frontiers. So it is not clear that bringing jobs to the developing (and the East European) countries is necessarily an alternative to bringing workers to the industrial countries. Clearly, this is not an argument against liberalising trade and capital flows with the South and East, which is in the self-interest of the North, nor is it an argument against giving aid.

It has been estimated that roughly 80 million people live in countries they were not born in.[101] An additional 20 million live abroad as refugees from natural disasters or political oppression. These are large numbers by historical standards, though small compared with the much larger populations of the countries of immigration. The USA is the largest recipient of migrants: nearly 800,000 in 1997, down from nearly 2 million in 1991. Germany had 800,000 immigrants in 1994 and 1995, but this figure includes many temporary workers.[102]

---

[100] Robert Schoeni, Kevin McCarthy and George Vernez (undated).

[101] Peter Stalker (1994).

[102] *The Economist* (1997) p. 81 and U.S. Census Bureau, *Statistical Abstract of the United States (1999).* P. 2.

The debate about the benefits and damage of the brain drain, or the selective outflow of professional people trained in a low-income country to a higher- income country, has distinguished between three groups: the migrants, those they join, and those they leave behind. It is usually agreed that the first two groups gain from brain drain. Controversy arises over the third.

On the one side there are those who point to benefits of the free movement of human beings. Above all, the migrating individual and her (always, and more frequently, including his) family gain. In addition, the contribution to knowledge of the migrant is often greater abroad, because better facilities for her work are available. The greater contribution which she makes to knowledge is often available to the whole world.

Occasionally she returns, after a period of self-improvement, to her own country; while away, she may send remittances to her family at home. And, although she is depriving her country of taxable capacity, she relieves it of burdens such as educating her children. Her home country may enjoy political benefits and prestige from having ex-nationals (if they have not been driven out), in positions of power and influence. Worldwide living standards are improved by permitting talent to go to its highest-yielding activity, and equality is promoted by the weakening of monopoly positions.

While this cosmopolitan line of reasoning has appeal, some qualifications are necessary.

First, the home country has borne (some of) the costs of educating the migrant, but loses the tax revenue from her income.

Second, there are intellectual as well as technical economies of scale, external economies and complementarities. The emigration of leading professionals (e.g. teachers) can (a) deprive those left behind of guidance and stimulus. And there is (b) the loss of employment opportunities for less highly trained people, such as assistants. Migration of professional people can therefore impoverish the lower income groups in the developing countries.

Third, the problem is aggravated by the fact that the mobility is partial. Trained and skilled manpower moves, while unskilled and semi-skilled people move much less. While it may be best to permit both skilled and unskilled to move freely, it does not follow that any step towards greater freedom of movement is good. If the skilled can move and the unskilled cannot, it may be better to restrict also the movement of the skilled.

Fourth, possibly the most important impact of the brain drain, or rather of attempts to plug it, is the impact on internal income distribution. In order to prevent skilled people from leaving, salary differentials have to be raised and an initial inegalitarian income distribution is reinforced or aggravated. This adds obstacles to national integration, and retarded development adds to the temptations of the brain drain. This creates additional incentives to inequalities, and so on in a vicious circle.

Fifth, the external brain drain is matched by an internal drain: the reference group for the poor country professionals is the group of their peers in the rich countries. For example, doctors go to the cities to practise expensive, private, curative medicine instead of to rural areas where they could render more useful preventive, low-cost health services.

Many policy options have been discussed, including a special tax on professional migrants that would be collected by their host country and remitted to their country of origin.

15. East Asia versus the rest of the South

It is generally agreed that East Asia, on balance, benefited from globalisation, whereas Africa (with some exceptions such as Mauritius and Botswana) and Latin America (with some exceptions such as Chile, Costa Rica and Bolivia) lost. Until 1997 the East Asian countries were held up as models for other developing countries. Since the crisis many critics have condemned them for their unworkable economic systems. Joseph Stiglitz has written: "This dramatic swing in opinions about the Asian development model, matching the dramatic changes in the markets, has gone further than is justified by the fundamentals. No other economic system has delivered so much, to so many, in so short a span of time."[103]

Could the successful experience of East Asia be generalized? It has been argued that the export-orientation of East Asia has contributed to its success, but that it would be fallacious to apply this experience to all developing countries. It must, however, be remembered that an import-substitution phase preceded the phase of successful exports. But exports tend to be exposed to more competition, and their production therefore tends to be more efficient. Firms can learn in international markets and the foreign contacts help entering related markets. For these reasons East Asian governments have encouraged exporting, and this is regarded as partly responsible for their success. They have done this by providing infrastructure, by preferential access to credit and foreign exchange, by providing information about foreign markets, and by improving the quality and enhancing the reputation of exports. Can this experience be generalised to other developing countries?

If all developing countries matched Taiwan's or South Korea's proportion of the labour force or GDP in exports, the need to absorb a vastly larger volume of exports would run into difficulties. It is, of

---

[103] Joseph Stiglitz (1998).

course, true that the extra revenue earned by these exports would be spent on extra imports. The phasing of trade liberalization would be different for different countries, and not all exports would be dumped onto world markets simultaneously. The commodity composition and the export/GDP ratios would also be different for different countries and at different times. Many developing countries would continue to export primary products. Since labour-rich, resource-poor developing countries like the East Asian "tigers" are likely to have a larger proportion of their labour force in exports than resource-rich, labour-poor (relatively to land[104]) countries like Brazil and Argentina, the impact on world markets and employment would be reduced. Some exports would be directed at other developing countries whose vested interests are less strong in clamouring for protection. And, as a result of trade liberalisation, counter-protectionist pressure groups in the rich industrialised[105] countries, such as agriculture in the United States, would gain in strength.[106]

All these considerations would soften the impact of the extra exports. But in spite of these mitigating circumstances, there are bound to be serious adjustment problems in the importing countries. If growth rates are sluggish and unemployment is high, protectionist barriers are likely to go up, or the terms of trade are likely to deteriorate for the exporters of manufactures.

Taiwan, Singapore and Hong Kong could create, at an earlier stage, many jobs by labour-intensive exports because they are small countries in whose economy foreign trade plays a large part. India and Brazil, on the other hand, have to devote the bulk of their efforts to designing and adapting technologies, processes and products for their vast domestic markets. Globalisation has not been equally helpful, and may in some instances have been damaging, to these efforts.

---

[104] Obviously this does not mean that Brazil has absorbed all its surplus labour: only that land is plentiful.

[105] The term "industrialised" is no longer appropriate, since they have become largely service economies. "Advanced" may be misinterpreted as dismissing the cultural characteristics of poorer countries as backward.

[106] China does, however, present a problem. China has not only plentiful cheap labour, but labour with the same ability as the East Asian tigers.

Dani Rodrick has questioned the importance attached to exports even in the success story.[107]

He shows that:

> "the increase in the relative profitability of exports around the mid-1960s was modest [in South Korea and Taiwan] and can account fully neither for the initial jump in the export-GDP ratio at that time nor for the subsequent steady increase in that ratio.
>
> A much more plausible explanation for the economic take-off is the sharp increase in investment demand that took place in the early 1960s....[I]n the early 1960s and thereafter the Korean and Taiwanese governments managed to engineer a significant increase in the private return to capital. They did so not only by removing a number of impediments to investment and establishing a sound investment climate, but more importantly by alleviating a coordination failure which had blocked economic take-off. The latter required a range of strategic interventions - including investment subsidies, administrative guidance and the use of public enterprise - which went considerably beyond those discussed in the standard account. That government intervention could play such a productive role was conditioned in turn by a set of advantageous initial conditions: namely, a favourable human capital endowment and relatively equal distribution of income and wealth" (p. 57).

Finally, there is the different role played by the government. It is now generally agreed that South Korea and Taiwan did not achieve their success by laissez-faire. The invisible hand of the market was guided by the highly visible and strong arm of the state. The financial crisis that started in 1997 was the result of premature and excessive deregulation, especially of short-term borrowing from abroad and inadequate bank regulation. Banks and manufacturing firms borrowed in dollars and invested recklessly at home when regulations were removed, and were unable to meet their obligations when the Korean currency fell. Thailand, for example, used to have restrictions on bank

---

[107] Dani Rodrick (1995) pp. 55-107.

lending to real estate. In the process of liberalisation it got rid of these restrictions without establishing a more sophisticated regulatory regime.[108] The relations between governments, banks and firms were sometimes corrupt, often incompetent.

Japanese, European and American banks were also at fault in lending eagerly in spite of evidence of possible defaults. The different financial structures in the East Asian economies also contributed to the crisis. Ratios of debt to equity of firms are much higher in Japan and South Korea than in the USA and Britain. At the end of 1996 the top 30 chaebol had an average debt-equity ratio of 400 per cent, compared with 70 per cent in the USA. As a result, they are subject to much higher risks. There is growing consent that governments should regulate short-term capital inflows. In order to discourage lenders, defaults should occasionally be permitted, so that both borrowers and lenders know that they will not be bailed out.

Has there been contagion? Were sound economies elsewhere affected by what happened in East Asia through shocks from abroad resulting from falling exports, rising imports and withdrawals of capital? If so, policies to curb the infection become an international public good. Some economists insist that there has not been contagion. Every country suffers capital withdrawal for its own reasons. Others maintain that changes in perceptions about the creditworthiness of a borrower and willingness to lend can spread from one area to others. In a crisis-free world countries will receive funds that would be withdrawn when crises in other places make the world a gloomier place. And obviously the infection can spread through falls in the demand for exports and higher pressures to import.

The global crisis that originated in East Asia has thrown 20 million Asians back into poverty in 1998, made 40 per cent of the Russian population poorer than ever and produced growing unemployment in Brazil, a country in which inequalities between rich and poor are among the greatest in the world.

The issue is no longer government intervention versus laissez-faire, but efficient and encouraging forms of intervention versus restricting and crippling ones. It is not even a question of general, market-friendly interventions versus selective ones. The countries cited as shining examples of free markets have powerfully intervened in the allocation of investment, steering the private sector by differential

---

[108] Joseph Stiglitz (1998).

interest rates, using a battery of import controls and export incentives, not only selecting, but creating winners (such as steel and ship-building without their natural resource base in South Korea) and cultivating a large and efficient public sector.

The South Korean public-sector Pohang Steel Company (POSCO) is one of the most efficient public enterprises in the world, while the Steel Authority of India is a testimony to bureaucratic inefficiency. The Korean firm has financial autonomy, seeks to make profits, has clear objectives, has operating independence, and is open to potential competition from domestic rivals and imports. The Indian Authority accepts losses and has confusing objectives, its finances overlap with the budget, it is subject to close political scrutiny and interference, its prices are politicized, and it is protected from competition through tariffs, import licensing, and legal restrictions on domestic entry. In 1986 the Steel Authority of India "paid 247,000 people to produce some 6 million tons of finished steel, whereas 10,000 South Korean workers employed by the Pohang Steel Company produce 14 million tons that same year.[109]

The success of the East Asian economies was bought at the price of heavy pollution. No area of the world has cities with worse air pollution and dirtier rivers and lakes. Unless governments do something about these problems they threaten the sustainability of the region's prosperity.

Paul Krugman and others have argued that the high growth rates were the result of abundant labour and capital. The argument is based on the work of Alwyn Young. Once these abundant factors of production were exhausted, growth would slow down. Like Stalin's Soviet Union, accumulation, not growth of factor productivity, caused the appearance of a miracle. As the temporary crisis of 1997-98 showed, too many investors and borrowers thought that the rapid growth rates would continue for ever. The East Asian economies remain high-savings, high productivity, low-inflation, low-budget deficits societies with a strong work ethic and discipline that promise recovery.

It is sometimes said that the government interventions in East Asia were carried out by skilled, well-trained, flexible, relatively non-corrupt public servants, with clear objectives, in consultation with the private sector, and that other developing countries do not have such

---

[109] Shashi Tharoor (1997).

bureaucrats and should therefore refrain from similar policies. But capability is not destiny. The correct conclusion surely is that they should emulate the training, skills, clear objectives, and detachment of the public servants of these model countries and create similar civil services themselves. Admittedly, this is a slow process, but it will yield results in the long run. There is no single East Asian model. An initial land reform, massive investment in human capital, especially mass education, encouragement of physical investment and technological progress, promotion of exports, creation of incentives, prescriptive rather than proscriptive government interventions, clear objectives for public enterprises, macroeconomic stability, these are some of the ingredients, in the right mixture, of their success in making good use of globalisation.

16. Global governance

Globalisation has proceeded at a rate faster than global government. The power of national governments and their ability to make national policies and pay for social services has been reduced without a corresponding increase in supra-national government or effective international cooperation. Other causes were at work too. Many countries became committed to unsustainable levels of expenditure at moderate rates of economic growth; populations were aging, health costs rising, etc. Welfare expenditures and subsidies for the poor have been cut and/or privatised, so that those who cannot afford to pay have to do without them. The result of this lag of political institutions behind globalising technology and liberalisation is a loss in the capacity to govern. Karl Polanyi wrote that the national market was embedded in society and the state, but no such authority governs the international market.[110] Government interventions are necessary in order to make the market work: safety nets, social insurance, unemployment assistance, adjustment assistance, retraining programmes, competition policy, infrastructure, health and safety regulations, research and development are examples. In the early 20th century, when capitalism and free markets were at their height, the government stepped in with minimum wage, child labour and workplace safety laws. The state promoted the public good of the market while combating and compensating for the public bads that it entails. But we do not have the global equivalent; at the global level the market reigns supreme. There are no global regulations, no policies, no protection, no safeguards, no competition policy. National governments are in retreat, reducing social services, tax bases and safety nets, though the rhetoric is ahead of actual actions. While global forces reduce the power of people to influence policy democratically at the

---

[110] Karl Polanyi (1944) I owe this argument to Mohan Rao. See also Mohan Rao (1995). The expression "embedded liberalism" for the postwar bargain between trade liberalisation and social government policies is due to John G. Ruggie (1995) pp. 507-526.

national level, at the global level, where the need now is greater, there are no democratic institutions and in many areas no institutions at all, that would enable people to control or even influence their destiny.

The vacuum has been filled to some extent by the multinational corporations. Corporate managers, not citizens, are the new policy makers. But the spread of these companies and of international financial capital has led to the complaint that national economies are no longer governable, while the global economy is ungoverned. Whatever embryonic global political institutions exist are not democratically controlled and people do not consider them as representing their interests, their views, or their values. But government is not the same as governance.

"Global governance" and "the international community" are words that can be used to conceal rather than reveal meanings. Many sins are committed in the name of "global governance" and the "international" or "global community." They are part of diplomacy by language, used to "dignify the sordid processes of international politics."[111] We read of the business community, the black community, the gay community, and, of course, of the international community. Once upon a time it was a word with a meaning. As *The Economist* has pointed out, we spoke of Anabaptists, or Mormons, or Benedictine monks or Oneida as communities. Now it is a tetrasyllabic mouthful attached to everything and signifying nothing. Perhaps the most pernicious community of all is the international one. Regularly invoked, constantly cited, endlessly expected to sort out or to "address" (as the current phrase has it[112]) every mess in every country, you might think that such a thing as the international community actually existed. It doesn't. There is something called the United Nations and numberless other bodies that try, for better or worse, to promote economic development, settle refugees, heal the sick, feed the hungry and count the dead. But it is not a community. In addition to the society of states there are special interest groups consisting of diplomats, members of international organisations and of the world of business, international finance and communications, and humanitarian activists.

Similarly "governance." It was politically difficult to complain about corruption, mismanagement, and the abuses of authoritarian

---

[111] George Orwell (1946) quoted in Göran Ohlin (1994).

[112] How were problems solved, issues tackled, and questions answered before all were addressed? That was a fate reserved to envelopes. The pretentious use of the word is taken from golf jargon.

regimes, especially in Africa, without giving offence. So a new term was invented whose meaning in relation to the more old-fashioned "government" is not clear. Kenneth Minogue writes: "I myself am not keen on the term 'governance,' because its recent revival seems to me, rather sinisterly, to express the oligarchic interest in removing the idea of will from the activity of government. Ruling turns into a process of notionally consensual mnanagement."[113] The American Heritage Dictionary defines governance as "the act, process or power of governing; government;" the Oxford English Dictionary as "the act or manner of governing, of exercising control or authority over the actions of subjects; a system of regulations." The International Encyclopedia of the Social Sciences has no entry for "governance," nor does the word appear in its index.

K. Sawar Lateef says that the World Bank defines governance as "the manner in which power is exercised in the management of a country's economic and social resources for development,"[114] while Edgardo Boeninger defines governance as "the good government of society."[115] Pierre Landell- Mills and Ismail Serageldin define it as "denoting how people are ruled, and how the affairs of a state are administered and regulated. It refers to a nation's system of politics and how this functions in relation to public administration and law. Thus the concept of governance includes a political dimension."[116] A World Bank report on Africa defined governance as the "exercise of political power to manage the nation's affairs."[117] Addressing (this time really) a joint meeting of bankers and business associations in Manila on 18 October 1994, Michel Camdessus defined good governance, the fifth of his conditions "for achieving high-quality growth" (those were the good old days) as "government that serves the whole of society rather than sectional interests."[118] The World Bank and the International Monetary Fund have replaced "getting prices right by "getting governance right." Joan Nelson distinguishes between three elements of governance: democracy, good government, and development.[119] Perhaps the widest definition of governance is given in the Report of

---

[113] Kenneth Minogue (2000) p. 30.
[114] K. Sawar Lateef (1992) p. 295.
[115] K. Sawar Lateef (1992).
[116] Pierre Landell-Mills and Ismail Serageldin (1992) pp. 303-320.
[117] World Bank (1989).
[118] *IMF Survey* (1994) p. 300.
[119] Joan Nelson (1992) p. 289.

the Commission on Global Governance "Our Global Neigh-bourhood."[120] "Governance is the sum of the many ways individuals and institutions, public and private, manage their common affairs. It is a continuing process through which conflicting or diverse interests may be accommodated and co-operative action may be taken. It includes formal institutions and regimes empowered to enforce compliance, as well as informal arrangements that people and institutions either have agreed to or perceive to be in their interest."[121] What then is global governance? "When the nation-state is no longer able to solve a host of urgent problems by its own efforts, it should, out of enlightened self-interest, seek an order that promises to restore some power of action to it. This attempt to tackle global problems is called global governance."[122] Global governance does not mean world government, nor the sum of the activities of states. It refers to the cooperation and interaction of states, private sector firms, national and global civil society, multilateral institutions, regional agents and local politics.

The late Göran Ohlin wrote in the context of international cooperation, "what some may have in mind is a vague notion of something less than government but more than chaos - regimes of the kind that already exist for many purposes."[123] But one could also interpret it as meaning more than government: including not only global, central, provincial (or, in a federation, state) and local government, but also relations with the civil society, the private profit-seeking sector, the market, the family, and the individual citizen, in so far as these relations bear on governing a society. That civil society and civic culture (as it has evolved through hundred years) are particularly important for good governance is shown for Italy by Robert D. Putnam's wonderful book *Making Democracy Work.*[124] He shows that what he calls civic "norms and networks of social engagement" facilitate the working of democracy. The social capital of trust and reciprocity that is invested in norms and networks of civic life is seen as a vital factor of effective government and economic progress. That the market is an important institution of governance does not need stressing nowadays. Cultural factors, too, determine, as well as are determined by, governance.

---

120 The Report of the Commission on Global Governance (1995) p.2.

121 The Commission on Global Governance *Update* (1994) p. 3.

122 Dirk Messner and Franz Nuscheler (1996).

123 Göran Ohlin (1994).

124 Robert D. Putnam with Robert Leonardi and Raffaela Y. Nanetti (1993).

There is an important international civil society that cuts across national boundaries: private voluntary associations, churches, religious communities, professional organizations, international trade unions, interest groups, citizens' groups, grassroots organisations, action groups, etc. although they do not wield ultimate authority. More recently women's groups, environmentalists, human rights organisations, etc. are a global response to the deleterious impact of globalisation. They, too, can commit their members. Civil society, too, is being globalised. Of course, they represent the particular interests and values of their members. These may conflict with wider global interests and values. And there are the already mentioned multinational corporations and international banks. How can the UN agencies and other international and regional organisations become more responsive to the demands and needs of the global civil society and more participatory? We hear a lot about the need for greater participation, but the international organisations preaching this gospel have not been outstanding in practising what they preach. It has something to do with the blind spot of auto-professionalism, a subject on which I keep a secret file. It contains facts and reflections about dentists' children having bad teeth, marriage guidance counsellors suffering from broken marriages, management experts being unable to manage their own affairs, evaluators never evaluating their own activities, and the auditors of the Royal Economic Society having to refuse to audit its books.

Civil society can create and guarantee human security, as well as threaten and destroy it. Unattractive representatives of the civil society are the National Rifle Association or the Ku Klux Kan or the Mafia. A powerful civil society faced by a weak state can also destroy society, as it has done in pre-1989 Lebanon, Sri Lanka and the former Yugoslavia. There has been a shift from conflicts between states to conflicts within civil societies. Threats of environmental degradation, ethnic and religious conflicts, famine, poverty, population growth, disease, drugs, terrorism, crime, migration, have replaced the threats from nuclear war.

17. Global social capital

While national social capital has received a good deal of attention, global social capital has been relatively neglected. Associations running across national frontiers include international NGOs, professional organizations, interest groups, churches, political alliances, Internet communities, international inter-governmental organizations such as the World Bank, the IMF, the United Nations and its agencies and profit-seeking multinational corporations. Do they contribute to global social, cultural or economic achievements? How are they related to national and sub-national social capital? How to global public goods?

Globalization and the formation of global social capital can come from above (multinational firms, multilateral institutions, world markets, international capital flows) or it can come from below (Greenpeace efforts to prevent Shell from sinking an oil rig with toxic properties in the North Sea; the campaign in the South Pacific to protest against the resumption of French nuclear weapons tests).[125] The protesters against globalization at Seattle, Washington and Prague present, paradoxically, an example of globalization from below. The end of the OECD's planned Multilateral Agreement on Investment in 1998 and of the Seattle meeting of the World Trade Organization were two of the movement's successes. The UNDP has a board of NGOs to advise the administrator on issues involving firms, governments and civil society.[126]

Several global conferences organized by the United Nations on women, population, the environment, development and social priorities, with their parallel events organized by NGOs, balancing and counteracting the intergovernmental aspects, have begun to show new

---

[125] See Richard Falk (1996) p. 58.

[126] This is not to say that the greater influence of unelected, unaccountable and unrepresentative NGOs is necessarily good. See Paul Streeten (1997) pp. 193-210.

styles of participation, accountability, and representation.[127] Though rudimentary, these beginnings may present a form of education for world citizenship. Institutions such as the regional development banks, various UN bodies and international NGOs can contribute to this process. The aim would be to produce patriotic cosmopolitans, people who combine loyalty to their families, communities and countries with solidarity to humanity as a whole.

The IMF, the World Bank and orthodox economists argue for full integration of the developing countries into the global economy. But we have seen that to achieve a human world order this must be accompanied by policies that guarantee the satisfaction of basic needs, that correct for highly unequal asset and income distribution, and that prevent the growth of insecurity and social exclusion. To bring 1.3 billion people now below the poverty line up to minimum level would call for a fourfold increase in current aid. We know that this is not likely to happen. The aid prospects look gloomy.

In addition to markets and states there are three influential actors on the global stage: transnational corporations, international organizations, and the global civil society. Transnational corporations have been praised for making the most valuable contributions to development and condemned as not perhaps the devil incarnate, but at any rate the devil incorporated. No doubt, they wield considerable power and are not under global control. And different corporations behave very differently. Their economic power is often greater than that of many states and their activities can affect the politics of governments and people. Ideally and eventually, a system of global incorporation, global taxation, and global accountability should match the global reach of these corporations. Meanwhile international (i.e. inter-governmental) cooperation will have to limit the abuse of their power and attempt to steer its use to the public good.

The United Nations and its agencies and other worldwide international and regional public agencies and organizations are specifically charged with promoting the general interest, including economic and social wellbeing, in different spheres. Here again, a greater degree of public control, accountability, transparency, and more particularly wider participation by voluntary societies, religious congregations, trade unions, private firms, professional organizations, women's and youth organizations, and so on would be desirable. It is

---

[127] Richard Falk (1996) p. 59.

these international agencies, together with the fledgling global civil society that are the seat of the global conscience of the world.

Last but not least there is the global civil society in the making, neither private nor public. The bonds of global non-governmental, non-profit organizations that draw on the voluntary energies of its members and contribute often highly efficiently not only to the gross national product but to a flourishing civil society and the social capital, essential for a democracy. They include voluntary societies, advocacy groups, grassroots organizations, churches and other religious associations, action groups, professional societies, colleges, universities, Oxfam, Bread for the World, Greenpeace, orchestras, hospitals, museums, the Red Cross, Friends of the Earth, Amnesty International, Greenpeace, charities, cooperatives, the Grameen Bank, neighborhood organizations, local action committees, and many others and similar institutions. They stretch across national frontiers and forge links that bypass national frontiers and loyalties. They have put issues on the agenda of governments and of public debate that may otherwise have been neglected: poverty, the environment, women's (and children's) rights and human rights, political freedom and governance, empowerment, corruption, the role of women (and children), population, habitation, the waste of military expenditure and the "peace dividend," debt relief for the poorest countries, and others. They constitute the core of any future world citizenship, even though their loyalties may be confined to quite narrow issues or special interests.

They can mobilize world opinion in order to draw attention to global problems, such as some environmental and human rights groups have done so successfully. Greenpeace on some environmental issues or Amnesty International on human rights or Oxfam on public education in development issues, as well as the execution of projects, can serve as examples. Other organizations provide humanitarian relief or engage in cooperation beyond state frontiers, for example by establishing links with local self-help groups and supporting their health, education or community projects.

Undeniably, non-state agents differ vastly in their capabilities and some of them appear to have hardly any influence at all. This seems to exempt them from any role in shaping a global civil society. Still, to the extent that they do have leverage within their specialized sphere of activity, they have a responsibility, and they must strive to make their own specific contribution to the realization of a global civil society.

Before the Prague meeting of the World Bank and the International Monetary Fund in the year 2000 the Bank's President, Mr. Wolfensohn, spent some time with non-governmental organizations including the Bolivian Episcopal Conference, the Coalition for Democracy and Civil Society of the Kyrgyz Republic, and a representative from World Vision from Uganda. The discussion ranged from corruption to the control of multinational corporations to the equitable division of the gains from the Chad-Cameroon oil pipeline. It was the first time that such a meeting took place. It is the beginning of the politics of a global economy.

Globalization has so far applied mainly to the free flow of trade, finance, technology, and some educational and cultural impulses in accordance with free market principles. The movement of people has been much less free. And the growth of institutions to protect the poor and the weak, to promote civil and human right, to provide educational and health facilities and social safety-nets, has lagged behind the drive of market forces. The result has been growing international inequality.

How can the UN agencies and other international and regional organizations become more responsive to the demands and needs of the global civil society and more participatory? We hear a lot about the need for greater participation, but the international organizations preaching this gospel have not been outstanding in practicing what they preach. It has something to do with the blind spot of auto-professionalism, a subject on which I keep a secret file. It contains facts and reflections about dentists' children having bad teeth, marriage guidance counselors suffering from broken marriages, management experts being unable to manage their own affairs, evaluators never evaluating their own activities, and the auditors of the Royal Economic Society having to refuse to audit its books.

We also have recently heard a good deal about the need to decentralize government and to draw more on participatory organizations in the political arena. The world has found unworkable and has rejected the process of centralized decision-making in centrally planned economies. But the very same process governs the relations between management and labor within both capitalist and public sector firms. We know that under regimentation people do not give their best. Democracy and participation should be introduced not only in politics but also in the private sector; and not only in government and in profit-seeking firms, but also in private voluntary societies and non-governmental organizations such as trade unions and churches; even in some families there is a need for greater participation, or at least better access to those in power, particularly by women and in some areas by children. This might be called vertical participation: to make the membership of these agencies more responsive to the needs of all its members through a higher degree of participation and access to power. By horizontal participation I mean the inclusion in the international organizations of some representatives of the civil society.

With the end of the Cold War, the role of the United Nations and its agencies can once again become what it was intended to be at its foundation, but with adaptation to the new power constellations and the new technologies of the present world. Japan and Germany must be given bigger roles. They should be encouraged to take positive initiatives in raising resources, and in the many activities surrounding various aspects of human security. Peace-keeping and peace-making applies to military and territorial security; ex-President Clinton talks of personal security (from conflicts, poverty- and drug-related crimes, violence against women and children, terrorism) and health security; food security is the mandate of the FAO; health security that of the World Health Organization; financial security that of the International Monetary Fund, the World Bank, and the regional development banks, environmental security that of the United Nations Environment Program and job and income security that of the ILO. Community security against ethnic and religious clashes and political security against the violation of human rights should be added to the list. The creation of productive, remunerative, secure, satisfying, freely chosen livelihoods should be a top priority for policy makers.[128]

Human security can often be increased not by increasing but by reducing defence expenditure. Ethnic conflicts, civil wars, external aggression and genocide have frequently economic and social roots in the extreme human insecurity that arises from hunger, poverty, unemployment, discrimination, social exclusion and cultural disintegration. Tackling the root causes of poverty, exclusion and racial and religious conflicts by preventive action - rather than by intervention after conflicts have broken out into open wars - can be much more effective and save many lives.

---

[128] It should be noted that what some regard as benefits others regard as threats to competitiveness and therefore welfare. For instance, job security, guaranteed old age pensions and a comprehensive welfare programme may be regarded as contributing to human security, but also as adding to "inflexibility" and hence to social costs.

There is also global antisocial capital at work. Sophisticated, well-connected networks of criminals are a real and growing national security threat. There is a rise of transnational syndicates that know no boundaries to their illicit activities. The Clinton administration produced a report, released by the National Security Council in December 2000, that describes how Russian, Chinese, Nigerian, Middle Eastern and Italian gangs have enthusiastically embraced globalisation and technology to expand their domains and escape the police. Among their activities are terrorism, the illegal drug trade, alien smuggling, trafficking in women and children, copyright violations, money laundering, auto theft, paedophilia, and others. Diversified organized crime has become intertwined with the political élites in some countries. Some of these organisations are simultaneously engaged in legitimate activities such as building highways, while trading heroine. They may, of course, be regarded as negative aspects of the private profit-seeking sector rather than as antisocial capital. But the loyalties, bonds and honor among thieves resemble those that are evident in social capital. "All the wondrous developments of the new economy – falling costs, fewer borders, easy communications – help international terrorists and criminals as much as they do businessmen,"[129] In December 2000 a high-level conference was convened in Palermo, at which a Convention against Transnational Organized Crime was opened for signature. Military, economic and political power will have to meet the new threat.

Some libertarians (such as Mrs. Thatcher) were eager to destroy the desirable civil society, both local and global, while reformers in societies in which it has been destroyed (such as Mr. Gorbachev) had tried to rebuild it. Russia and some of the East European countries are still suffering from the absence of the trust and the institutions that a flourishing civil society creates. But here again, as in the case of the complementarity of private and public activities, the strength of the civil society and of NGOs in particular often lies not in opposing the public sector, but in cooperating with it, whether for finance, or for replication of successful ventures, or for support in opposing exploitative local power élites. In this way the state can contribute to the formation of social capital. In other circumstances, for example when faced with a predatory state, which would, unhindered, detract from social capital, their function is to combat it. But at the global level

---

[129] Fareed Zakaria (2000) p. 9.

there are no corresponding governmental and regulatory institutions to cooperate with (or oppose) the fledgling global civil society. Apart from inter-national (not global) institutions there are only global corporations and global NGOs.

18. Globalisation and international cooperation

In spite of the gloomy prospects for aid, there are five hopeful signs for global anti-poverty policies in the present climate.

First, the austerity programmes imposed mainly by the Fund have made political leaders receptive to more "targeted" programmes, protecting, or even advancing some of the more vulnerable groups. (We should avoid expressions like "targeting" and "target groups;" they suggest, in line with the Bank's military metaphors, people who are not only got at, but also shot at. But they have come to be widely accepted.) In the past these leaders had been keener on large-scale industrialization and infrastructure projects and had dismissed the informal sector as a disguised form of unemployment, not as a source of productive growth. Examples of the change are India's Integrated Rural Development Programme, Kenya's having begun to pay attention to the ILO report and Egypt's encouragement of small entrepreneurs. Shortly after the new President James Wolfensohn had taken over in the summer of 1995, the Bank cancelled a large hydroelectric project in Nepal after having referred it to a newly set up independent inspection panel. It is also scrutinizing other large-scale projects.

Second, the perhaps no longer quite so fashionable slogan of "getting prices right" can be used to benefit the informal sector, which, though it comprises, as we have seen, some quite well-off people, also contains many poor people. Low interest rates have often meant rationing in favour of large firms and depriving the informal sector of funds; and encouraging capital-intensive methods of production. High wages have often raised unemployment and helped only a privileged labour aristocracy. Low prices of publicly supplied electricity have helped private industry and the middle class; and so on. Devaluation of overvalued exchange rates can help the sales of informal sector enterprises. Kenya has about five years ago begun to give a tariff rebate for imported inputs to small manufacturers. The popularity of

Hernando de Soto's book *The Other Path* among high officials in the Republican Party, including ex-President Bush and ex-President Nixon, is a sign of the apparent convergence of business interests and anti-poverty concerns. In fact, the message of this book does not quite fit the Republican philosophy. For example, there is much more cooperation and mutual support in the informal sector than the individualistic, competitive ethos of private enterprise.

Third, problems caused by a balance of payments crisis and the need to service debt can also be helpful to the poor in the informal sector. By restraining imports, they direct demand to the products and services supplied by the informal sector. Devaluations may even encourage exports from the informal sector and if other exports are produced labour-intensively, this will help employment. The rise in the prices of imported inputs may make it worthwhile for large domestic firms to subcontract to informal sector firms.

Fourth, the current fashion for decentralisation, though it can in some cases reinforce the grip of local power elites who grind the faces of the poor and can shift financial responsibilities from the centre to local authorities, can also in other circumstances strengthen the access to political power of the poor, be more responsive to their needs, reduce corruption, and enhance equity and efficiency.

Fifth, the same is true of the fashionable switch to elevating the role of non-governmental organisations (NGOs), private voluntary organisations (PVOs) and cooperatives, and the move against large state bureaucracies. The Grameen Bank in Bangladesh, the Indian Self-Employed Women's Association based in Ahmedabad and the dairy project in Andhra Pradesh ("Operation Flood"), following the Anand model (Anand, in the state of Gujarat, is now the centre of the Indian dairy cooperatives), are outstanding successes in helping the poor through cooperative self-help. Since the late 1980s the World Bank has relied increasingly on NGOs as partners in planning and carrying out projects. In the period 1973-1988 NGOs were involved in only 6 per cent of total World Bank-financed projects. By 1990 NGOs were making a direct contribution to 22 per cent, and by 1998-1999 in 54 per cent of all Bank-financed projects. Interaction with NGOs is encouraged not only in the implementation but also in the design and planning of projects. There has also been increasing involvement with NGOs from the developing countries in the Bank's projects. Whereas in 1973-91 40 per cent of NGOs were international, by 1998 community-based organisations represented 70 per cent, local NGOs 80 per cent, and international NGOs only 25 per cent. (Often, an NGO falls into more than one category.) NGOs are also increasingly involved in macro-level consultations over Country Assistance Strategies, economic and sector work, public sector monitoring (e.g. public expenditure and the disbursement of aid) and Mr. Wolfensohn's Comprehensive Development Framework. In July 1995 an initiative was announced that could further enhance the role of NGOs. The Consultative Group to Assist the Poorest (CGAP) is, according to the Bank, designed "to promote the replication and growth of NGO-managed programs that provide financial services to the poor." The Bank has provided an initial capital of $30 million and other donors are expected to contribute at least as much. There is much more discussion of policies between NGOs and the Bank.[130] There is a seven member Policy Advisory Group (PAG), chaired by Dr. Muhammad Yunus of the Grameen Bank. Other members include Mrs. Ela Bhatt of the Self-Employed Women's Association and Nancy Barry of Women's World Banking.

In these ways the lot of poor people can be improved almost incidentally and as the result of the side-effects of strategies advocated by the Fund and Bank, though not in all cases with this explicit intention.

---

[130] Overseas Development Institute Briefing Paper (1995).

19. Human Adjustment Assistance and Social Conditionality

Monetary, fiscal, exchange rate and trade policies have been conventionally the content of conditionality. More recently, environmental, political and human rights policies have been added, without, alas, adding to the funds committed or disbursed. By a simple extension, human or social conditions deserve to be considered. It can be argued that these should have higher priority, because the effects of economic variables are not a matter of scientific certainty, whereas the obligation to reduce human misery is a moral certainty.

The UNDP and the chief architect of the annual Human Development Reports 1990-1996, the late Mahbub ul Haq, have eloquently put the case for human development. Globalisation has been discussed in terms of markets and in terms of states, but rarely in terms of its impact on people. Similarly, aid conditionality should be concerned with the impact of aid on people.

Two types of human conditionality, serving the objective of human development, may be considered. The first applies to the equivalent of adjustment assistance for the short-run transition period; the second to longer-term policies for human development.

A reform-minded government that wishes to implement a land reform, or a tax reform, or an educational reform, or an administrative reform, or to channel more resources into social services, or directly to the poor, may run into transitional difficulties, and is bound to impose additional burdens on the budget and on administration. If incomes are redistributed to the poor, the demand for food will rise. Food is likely to be in inelastic supply, so that inflationary pressures will increase. A land reform is likely to reduce food supplies in the short run. As more food imports are sucked into the country, the balance of payments will worsen and inflationary pressures will increase. As the incomes of the rich are reduced, unemployment in the luxury trades will increase. A combination of inflation and rising unemployment will result.

If the private sector loses confidence, there is likely to be capital flight, aggravating the balance of payments crisis. Domestic investment may decline, and security prices may fall. This would lead to a fall in the value of collateral for bank loans, could cause a banking crisis, and aggravate the decline in real investment. Disaffected groups may organise strikes, sabotage or even coups d'état. All these are familiar problems for radical governments that wish to change the course of policy in favour of the poor.

Unfortunately, the manifestations of such transitional difficulties look very much like the manifestations of a mismanaged economy. Indeed, if the reform-minded government has no experience, some degree of mismanagement will be added to the problems of the transition. In such critical situations, international donors can help make the transition less painful and disruptive, and increase the chances of success. Just as structural adjustment loans have been made to countries going through periods of economic restructuring of macro-economic policies, so *human adjustment assistance* should be adopted for countries taking positive steps towards human development. Such assistance would promote economic growth centred on people, by raising the nutrition, health, skills and productivity of the poor and by reducing population growth; and it would above all improve the human condition as a worthy end in itself.

The assistance could, for example, be used for investment in social infrastructure, such as clinics or schools. It could also help finance recurrent expenditure such as the salaries of teachers, healers, nurses, community workers, or purchasing medical or school supplies, or the materials for nutrition programmes. Assistance could also be used for activities that promote employment, including skill formation, training programmes and the provision of credit, encouraging micro-enterprises, or on building participatory institutions, and on strengthening indigenous capacity .

Like structural adjustment loans, human adjustment assistance would have to be based on a clear and well-defined strategy. Its progress should be carefully and objectively monitored, so that it is clear that the money achieves its intended objectives.

The principle of assisting human development could be extended from tiding over adjustment periods to long-term human and social development. What are the arguments for and against such a policy?

On the one hand, human conditionality may be regarded by recipient countries as intrusive and perhaps even violating national sovereignty. On the other hand, donors believe that their responsibility to the taxpayer is to account for the use of aid funds and to ensure that poverty reduction and human development are achieved, if this is the purpose of the aid. Donor institutions are distrusted by recipients, because they fear that extraneous criteria may enter into the process; and recipients' institutions are distrusted by donors, because they may wish to conceal unsuccessful performance. To resolve this conflict it is necessary to design institutions that are trusted by both sides, and monitor performance reliably and objectively.

In addition to having to gain the trust of both sides, and be responsive to their needs and demands, these institutions would have to fulfil the function of buffers between donors and recipients, would have to be sensitive to social and political conditions, and would have to have the expertise to judge the impact of programmes on poverty reduction. They should also be helpful in building up the indigenous capacity of poverty monitoring in developing countries.

One possible solution would be to adopt the method that the Organisation of European Economic Cooperation (OEEC), the forerunner of the OECD, practised under Marshall Aid. The USA generously withdrew from the process of monitoring the fulfillment of the conditions and encouraged European governments to monitor each other's performance. Analogously, groups of countries, such as those of East Africa, would get together, and one, say Uganda, would monitor the performance of another, say Kenya or Tanzania, and vice versa. Technical assistance would initially be needed to acquire or strengthen the professional capacity to do this.

Another solution would be to appoint a mutually agreed council of wise men and women, with a competent secretariat, who would be performing the monitoring, possibly again combined with technical assistance for the strengthening of indigenous capacity.

A third solution would be to aim at the creation of a genuine global secretariat, with loyalties to the embryonic world community, socially sensitive, and at the same time technically competent. The secretariats of existing international organisations such as the World Bank and the agencies of the United Nations have not quite reached that point, and are not perceived by recipients as being truly global in their loyalties and commitments. Reforms in recruitment, training, and promotion would be needed, and perhaps in the governance and location of these institutions. Decentralisation to strong regional offices,[131] whose members would have daily contact with the officials and the ordinary people of the recipient countries, may be a necessary condition. Until such reforms are instigated, bilateral aid has certain advantages in terms of targeting and monitoring over multilateral aid. This is against the conventional wisdom, but remains true as long as the bureaucracies of the largely uncontrolled multilateral agencies are not reformed.

Whatever institutional solution might be adopted, there is virtue in introducing a degree of competition into the monitoring process, so that a variety of methods may be tested against each other. At the moment it is feared that the large international financial institutions exercise a monopoly of power and wisdom, and propagate at times the prematurely crystallized orthodoxies mentioned above. The proposed buffer procedures or buffer institutions would have the additional advantage that they would contribute to the building and strengthening of indigenous research and monitoring capacities of the recipient developing countries. For research on poverty, action against poverty, and human development tend to go together, as the investigations of Charles Booth and Seebohm Rowntree at the beginning of the century, and of Sidney and Beatrice Webb, of the World Bank and of the Specialised UN Development Agencies have shown.

There is a fourth way of combining non-intrusiveness, and respect for national sovereignty with human development, which does not depend on a buffer institution. Instead of imposing as a condition for receiving aid the desirable policies, donors judge which countries intend to pursue good policies, or show a genuine intention of adopting them, and quietly support these countries. These are neither the needy nor the speedy, because the former may not use the aid effectively and the latter do not need it, but the potential greatest improvers. This might be called the "quiet style in aid-giving," because it does not proclaim its intentions, and does not use heavy-handed performance criteria, which can cause acrimony and bad feelings. Instead, worthy candidates are selected and supported. The message will soon get spread, and the signals will convey to others that if they wish to get aid, they, too, will have to adopt reforms and the right policies. If there is a

---

[131] They should be regional, not national, in order to avoid the current mistakes that arise from narrowly national points of view. The latter have led to advising, say, Kenya to diversify out of coffee into tea, and Sri Lanka out of tea into coffee, when both coffee and tea are in world surplus.

dialogue that precedes the disbursements, it proceeds by persuasion, not by coercion.

Whatever form is adopted, it should be remembered that there are obligations on the side of both the recipient and the donor. It may therefore be more appropriate to move away from the language of conditionality and, by dialogue, towards the language of a social compact. The donor also accepts certain conditions, relating to the quantity, quality, regularity and predictability of aid.

Finally, there is the question of additionality in two senses. First, if social and human conditionality enters the picture, is this additional to other forms of conditionality, or does it take the place of other conditions? In the last few years all sorts of conditions were added to those relating to the ability to repay the loan. Macro-economic policy conditions (fiscal discipline, reduced budget deficits, financial liberalisation, exchange rate adjustment, privatisation, deregulation, property rights) then conditions about the environment (green conditionality), about good governance, including free multi-party elections, human rights, and the rule of law, about anti-poverty measures, about reduced arms expenditure, and, of course, now human and social conditionality.

Second, are the funds for meeting the social conditions additional to other financial flows? The acceptability of social and human conditionality by recipients will clearly depend on the answer to these two questions. But additionality of resources raises unanswerable questions. What matters is not whether the funds are additional to what they had been in the past, but whether they are additional to what they would have been in the absence of the conditions. And this is an unknown, perhaps unknowable, quantity.

20. Aid and public opinion

According to an American poll released in January 1995 by the Program on International Policy Attitudes at the University of Maryland 75 per cent of Americans believe that the US spends "too much" on foreign aid and 64 per cent want foreign-aid spending cut.[132] Apparently 11 per cent think it is all right to spend "too much" on aid. A different election night poll in 1994 showed that nearly half the voters believed that either welfare or foreign aid was the largest item in the federal budget. In fact they are two of the smallest items.[133]

Respondents were also asked how large a share of the federal budget goes to foreign aid. The median answer was 15 per cent; the mean answer was 18 per cent. Other recent polls, including a Harris Poll in November 1993, indicated that Americans thought the government devoted 20 per cent or more of its spending to foreign assistance. The correct answer is less than one per cent of the budget. The US government spends about $ 14 billion a year on foreign aid (including military assistance), out of a total budget of a trillion and a half. About half of this is devoted to human development programmes such as health, education and family planning and is administered by the Agency for International Development.

To the question about how much would be appropriate, the median answer was 5 per cent of the budget, five times the actual expenditure. A question about how much would be "too little" produced a median answer of 3 per cent - more than three times the level of current expenditure on aid. Similar overestimates of aid given have been registered in other aid-giving countries.

After the pollsters revealed to their subjects the correct answer to the question about how much (or, rather, how little) the US spends on aid, 35 per cent of the respondents still said they wanted it cut. As *The New Yorker* points out, "This poll is less interesting for what it shows

---

[132] *The New Yorker* (1995) pp. 4-5.
[133] Bob Herbert (1995).

about foreign aid than for what it shows about American democracy. It's not just that Americans are scandalously ignorant. It's that they seem to believe they have a democratic right to their ignorance. All over the country - at dinner tables, in focus groups, on call-in radio shows, and, no doubt, occasionally on the floor of Congress - citizens are expressing outrage about how much we spend on foreign aid, without having the faintest idea what that amount is."

Another, related, popular American myth is that the USA is more generous than other countries. The USA devotes 0.15 per cent of its GDP to foreign aid, far less than other advanced countries, and the figure has been steadily declining in recent years. About $ 44.00 of the taxes paid annually by an average American family goes to foreign aid. In Denmark the equivalent figure is $ 900.00. However, voluntary contributions to private organisations have continued to rise.

There is also the widespread impression that all aid is wasted and that America gets nothing for it. Senator Jesse Helms calls it throwing money down a "rat hole." This may be an inference from the waste of other forms of public expenditure. Although much of cold war aid, given for the wrong reasons, to the wrong countries, for the wrong projects, not surprisingly did not show any results, the successes of aid to health, education, family planning and rural development have by now been well documented. Clearly, more could be done for human development. At the Social Summit in Copenhagen the 20:20 target was discussed and accepted by some: 20 per cent of the domestic budget and 20 per cent of foreign aid should be devoted to priority human development areas. The record on reduced illiteracy, preventive health care and reduced fertility rates has been impressive. Perhaps one should not be surprised at the ignorance of the American public. According to another recent poll, 60 per cent of Americans were unable to name the President who ordered the nuclear attack on Japan, and 35 per cent did not know that the first atomic bomb was dropped on Hiroshima.[134]

At the same time, the University of Maryland poll found that a strong majority supported the values inherent in foreign aid and, on being presented with a breakdown of the actual spending, wanted to maintain or increase spending in most, but not all, areas. If democratic action should reflect the values of the public, aid has considerable support in America. It is reasonable to assume that if aid is reformed in

---

[134] Bob Herbert (1995).

the directions suggested above, support for it would substantially increase.

The current fashion is to emphasize trade and private foreign investment. And it is true that investments in and loans to small enterprises have been very successful. The Small Enterprise Assistance Funds, a Washington venture-capital fund established by the Atlanta-based charity CARE, is an interesting new form of hybrid organisation: These are non-profit groups funded by governments and charities that act like private investors. They use their profits for re-investing in new small firms. Larger organisation, such as the International Finance Corporation, part of the World Bank, the U.S. Overseas Private Investment Corporation, and the European Bank for Reconstruction and Development, have, of course, lent to the private sector for some time. These new institutional hybrids have an important function. On the other hand, they cannot replace more conventional forms of development aid.

First, they seek out the developing world's best performers and leave out those that need money most. According to the OECD, 80% of private money goes to only 20 countries. Private funds are not attracted to Tanzania or Sierra Leone; they have gone to Indonesia and Malaysia.

Second, they do not necessarily help the people who need it most: the potential workers rather than their employers. Third, investment in the social sectors, health, education, nutrition and family planning, are not commercial propositions, although they pay off handsomely for society as a whole. Fourth, the success of private enterprise depends on physical infrastructure, which again is often done better by public investment. And there is always the need for emergency aid, aid to the unemployed and unemployables, the victims of the competitive struggle, who tend to fall under the net of profitable investment.

21. Competitiveness

The notion of competitiveness between countries has had a few hard knocks. Paul Krugman has reminded us that it does not apply to the relationship between countries, as opposed to firms. In the competitive struggle, as in competitive sports, the gains of one are at the expense of another.[135] Not so between countries, where the gains of one can be shown to lead to gains of others. If abused, the notion can lead to calls for protection, which hurts almost everyone.

But countries do have different rates of economic growth of income, different growth rates of productivity, and different growth rates of living standards. It is widely agreed that the rule of law and clearly defined property rights, high savings and investment in physical and human capital, good education, flexible labour markets, good macroeconomic policies aiming at labour-intensive growth, and high levels of technology, management and infrastructure have important roles to play. Some would add the need for the redistribution of productive assets (particularly land) in countries where they are very unequally distributed. In brief, certain legal and political institutions and certain policies are more conducive to growth than others. Whether the openness of an economy to trade and investment is a cause of high growth and good export performance, or a consequence, or both, is controversial, but they are clearly linked. Most economists believe that openness is an important cause of growth.

Growing international competition is not solely the result of fewer barriers to trade. Another important cause is the accelerated pace of invention and innovation. As the ratio of GNP spent by high-income countries on R&D rises from 2 to 3 per cent and higher, social and technological change has accelerated in the last few decades. Today the

---

[135] This is not quite true. In conditions of oligopoly, firms work with suppliers, build alliances and thrive on trust and loyalty. Business is no longer a branch of warfare, and cooperation can pay off (sometimes at the expense of buyers or workers or the environment). In theory the assumption of perfect competition has been replaced by game theory. Though globalisation can increase competition, oligopoly obviously applies even more in the global than in the national arena.

time-lag between innovative idea, invention, engineering application
and commercial exploitation is much shorter than it used to be. The
time lag between the invention of the steam engine and the railway age,
or between the invention of the internal combustion engine and the
economic, social and cultural (not to say anything about sexual)
diffusion and revolution wrought by the motor car was measured in
generations; that between the invention of television, the microchip, the
jet engine, or even the zip fastener, their engineering and commercial
applications, and the intellectual and cultural transformations in their
train, is measured in years. The application of the discovery of the
structure of DNA to bio-engineering took only ten years. Faraday's law
of electro-magnetic induction was announced in 1835. The electric
dynamo was invented in 1881, but it took 40 years before companies
learned how to reorganise their factories efficiently around electric
power to take advantage of its flexibility. On the other hand, Bardeen
and Brittain announced the laws governing semi-conduction in the late
forties of the last century, and transistor application followed only five
years later. The lag in the application of laser technology was even
shorter. As Gore Vidal wrote, "Thanks to modern technology...history
now comes equipped with a fast-forward button."[136]

If the majority of economists are right, liberalisation should lead
to higher growth rates and more rapid improvements in living
standards. Yet the evidence for this is slender if not absent. Annual
growth rates of GDP per head in East and Southeast Asia were 6-8%
per year between 1986 and 1993; in Latin America and Sub-Saharan
Africa in the same period they were only 0.36 - 0.37% a year. Growth
in these areas remained elusive. The exceptionally good performers are
Chile and Costa Rica in Latin America, and Mauritius and Botswana in
Africa. Comparing the annual growth rates of GNP per head in the two
periods 1965-1980 and 1980-93, we get for all developing countries 4.6
and 4 per cent, (low-income countries excluding China and India 0.1
per cent instead of 4 per cent), for the OECD countries 3.9 and 1.6 per
cent.[137] Table 3 shows the growth rates enjoyed by the number of
countries in the period 1972 -81 and 1982-91 compared with the 1960-
71 average.

---

[136] Gore Vidal (1992). Ronald Dore has argued that technological change has been more important
than globalisation in promoting competition and changing the character of our societies. "Ralf
Dahrendorf, Quadrare il Cerchio, Comment" by Ronald Dore. Typescript.
[137] UNDP Human Development Report (1995) and Word Bank World Development Report (1995).

Even if it were true that liberalisation led to higher growth, one would have to examine the policies in the preceding period that laid the basis for the subsequent success. All successful liberalisers had pursued selective trade and industrial policies, laying the foundations for their good performance later.

There was, however, until 1996, a puzzle. Robert Solow said a few years ago that "you can see the computer revolution everywhere but in the productivity statistics." The introduction of the new information technology and the growth of new and more convenient services, particularly from the computer revolution, had, until 1996, not shown up in correspondingly higher growth figures. The average annual rate of hourly labour productivity growth in America's business sector has slowed down from 2.6 per cent in 1960-73 to around 1.5 per cent until about 1996. If the figures are correct, they also suggest growing inequality, as the benefits to the winners, some of them substantial, were partly at the expense of the losses of the losers. However, since 1996 American GDP and productivity have resumed their growth and since 1998 spectacularly so. Since 1996 real GDP has grown at an annual rate of nearly 4 per cent, labour productivity per hour has grown by 2.9 per cent between 1994 and 1999, unemployment has fallen to 4.3 per cent, the lowest level since the 1960s, and income inequality has been reduced. All this without signs of accelerating inflation, which has dropped in 1999 to 1.9 per cent, the lowest level in 35 years. Computers and information technologies must have made a contribution to this performance, though how much is disputed. The highest growth in productivity has occurred in firms that produce information technology, not in those that use it. Policies also helped in raising productivity. The elimination of the budget deficit and its transformation into a surplus, making room for private savings and investment, and astute monetary policy also played their part.

Many economists, including a report of a panel of economists to the US Congress,[138] have reminded us that the official figures overstate inflation and understate economic growth. Quality improvements (such as radial car tires that are safer and last longer than the old ones), new products (such as microwave ovens that did not exist 30 years ago), new features of old products (such as colour TV with 50 channels and VCRs), and new services (such as the installation of more automatic

---

[138] The Congressional Advisory Commission on the Consumer Price Index, whose chairman was Professor Michael Boskin.

teller machines by banks in outlying neighbourhoods) are not fully accounted for.[139] But the overstatement of inflation and hence the understatement of productivity growth applies as much to earlier periods as to recent ones and therefore cannot account for the slowing down of productivity growth before 1996.

Three-quarters of all computers are used in the service sector, and improvements in services such as medical procedures are notoriously difficult to measure. The value of speed, quality improvements, and customer service are often not captured by official statistics. According to these statistics, for example, a bank today is no more efficient than a bank was two decades ago. This makes no allowance for 24-hour automated teller machines, which benefit customers who no longer have to queue in long lines to be served by human tellers during regular banking hours.

Many non-market provisions, such as a healthier environment, or reduced crime rates, do not figure at all. Some of the contributions of computers have improved the quality of life, led to greater convenience, and higher consumption, without showing up in higher productivity. In so far as they do lead to higher productivity, the time span is long: we shall have to wait and see whether the computer skills acquired by the children of today will show up in their higher productivity when they join the workforce. Absorbing the innovations to which the computer gives rise will also take many changes in work practices and behaviour.

---

[139] It should, however, be remembered (it not always is) that many attractive goods have disappeared from the market, and many others have *deteriorated* in quality. The time it takes to get by car from my old college, Balliol, to Magdalen Bridge has greatly increased and the services derived from cars in terms of faster travel have been reduced as a result of congestion. Tomatoes have become inedible, plastic has replaced metal, air travel through inconvenient "hubs" has become more cramped, less convenient and less comfortable; and the quality of higher education has deteriorated. Shoddy manufactured items do not last as long as they used to and cannot be repaired because of design, materials and method of assembly; to say nothing of air and water pollution, growing crime and insecurity, and the decline in domestic production resulting from increasing labour-force participation of women.

It is also a fact that consumer goods that have dropped in cost have been luxury items (computers, audio equipment, cars and long-distance telephone calls). The products that have increased in cost have been those essential to low-income and young families (food, new homes and rent, college tuition, medical care, public transport and basic telephone service). Considering the large amount of effort and money that have been spent on investigating country-specific purchasing power comparisons, a fraction of this ought to be devoted to calculating income-specific price levels. A separate index for the elderly (rich and poor), the young, and for large and small families would be revealing.

Another explanation of the slow growth until 1996 is that computers represent only 2 per cent of the USA's capital stock, and less in other OECD countries, whereas railways in their heyday represented more than 12 per cent.[140] But if equipment used for gathering, processing and transmitting information is added, the total amounts to 12 per cent of the American capital stock, about the same as the railways at the peak of their development. And purchases of computers during the last few years come to nearly 20 per cent of capital investment.

Some observers believe that the enormous power of computers is often superfluous. "Research into a variety of sources is now easier thanks to the Internet but word processors have not made novels or news reports any better; nor have faster calculations made economic forecasting more accurate. One wonders whether all those urgent cellular phone calls from restaurants and cars have made business more efficient."[141] Even when not superfluous, much depends on how the technology is applied and how its application is managed. It has also been argued that the work of knowledge workers such as managers, executives, doctors, lawyers and teachers does not lend itself readily to computer-driven improvements in productivity. Finally, it could be the case that much expenditure on computer technology has been wasteful. Computer systems are often not subject to proper investment appraisal and are badly used.[142] On the other hand, it is hard to believe that computers have not greatly increased the productivity of retail and wholesale distribution. The Internet has replaced distributors by an electronic market place. The reduction in uncertainty in the economy must also have contributed to productivity growth.

However, since 1996 productivity growth has picked up. Between 1996 and 1999 productivity has grown annually by an average of 2 per cent, roughly twice the rate between 1973 and 1995.This acceleration may be a sign that the investment in computers and communication is finally paying off. Businesses are at last reaping the benefits of information technology. This may also be the explanation for the unprecedented combination of high growth, rising wages and low inflation that the US economy has witnessed until 2001. Some have concluded from the recent strong performance of the economy

---

[140] Louis Uchitelle (1996) and Daniel Sichel (1997) p. 72.

[141] Jeff Madrick (1998) p. 31 and Steve Lohr (1999).

[142] This is the argument made by Paul Strassman (1997) p. 72.

that the long-awaited computer revolution has at last arrived.[143] But even the higher recent growth rates are low compared with earlier periods. In the 1950ies and 60ies productivity grew by 3.5 per cent and 4 per cent a year. And there were brief periods such as that between 1982 and 1986 when labour productivity grew by 2.4 per cent a year, but this growth was not sustained. It is too early to judge whether the revolution has come.

---

[143] Jeff Madrick (1998).

22. The case for a quieter life

Sir John Hicks said that the best of all monopoly profits is a quiet life.[144] The effort to maximize profits by equating marginal returns is itself subject to diminishing marginal (psychic) returns. The free trade gospel, based on the doctrine of comparative advantage, bids us always to strive for higher incomes from the international division of labour. Information technology, it has been said, brings us nearer the textbook model of economics: it provides more information, reduces transaction costs, and removes barriers to entry. "Computers and advanced telecommunications help to make these assumptions [of perfect knowledge, zero transaction cost and absence of barriers to entry] less far-fetched."[145] But adjustments in response to changing comparative advantage are costly, and the need for these adjustments has been speeded up by the new technologies. They involve changing occupations, often changing residence, periods of unemployment and uncertainty, and generally upheaval and disruption, sometimes of whole communities.

In an international environment in which comparative advantage changes rapidly, trade policy can, as we have seen, become a policy for tramps: it imposes the imperative to move from one occupation to another, from one residence to another, not once or twice, but continually. The citizens of an already fairly rich country, or a like-minded group of such countries, may say: we already enjoy many earthly goods. We wish to forgo some extra income from international trade for the sake of a quieter life; for not having to learn a new trade,

---

[144] J. R. Hicks (1935).
[145] Pam Woodall (1996) p. 46.

for not being uprooted from our community. There is nothing irrational or "non-economic" in such a choice.[146]

It will, of course, depend upon how important international trade is in the economy of the country. It must avoid suffering reductions in income resulting from having opted out, even only at the margin, of remaining internationally competitive. It will also depend on not permitting the vested interests benefiting from the protection (which include capitalists and managers, as well as workers) to become so powerful as to drive the economy beyond the point where forgone income from international specialization just balances the benefits of a somewhat less disruptive life. It is probably true that many countries have sought protection beyond this optimum point, and the real costs to the community of keeping workers employed in industries that should be shrunk greatly exceeds the benefits that could be reaped by a redeployment of labour.

The qualification introduced above for countries heavily dependent on international trade would, in turn, have to be qualified if international cooperation could be implemented on the optimum rate of technical progress, where such progress involves disruption. As I have argued above, in most other lines of advance we accept the application of some form of benefit/cost calculus, but only where advances in knowledge and its technical and commercial application are concerned do we not ask questions about its social and human costs.

There is a literature on the so-called "non-economic" objectives of policy-makers, such as the desire to maintain a large agricultural sector (or industrial sector) as an end in itself, and on how to modify free trade policy to accommodate them.[147] But my point is not to introduce non-economic objectives. Leisure is part of conventional economic objectives, as is avoiding the psychological and financial costs of disruption: the costs of resettlement, of rehousing, of

---

[146] The poor, unskilled, slow learners in the rich countries are particularly likely to be hit by trade liberalisation. Professionals, skilled workers, producers of sophisticated services like finance can readily adapt to changing conditions. Another option would be to train a force of workers who must be ready to move to new places and learn new skills in response to the changing international scene. These 'commandos' would get higher pay and better conditions than the ordinary work force in return for accepting these disruptions. The life might appeal to young bachelors or people keen on frequent change. But, as Ronald Dore, has pointed out, with the reduced importance of unskilled and semi-skilled labour, and the growing importance of highly skilled people, retraining is difficult or impossible.

[147] Among the contributors to this literature in the 1950s and 1960s are Max Corden, Harry Johnson, Jagdish Bhagwati, and T. N. Srinivasan

retraining, etc. These benefits and costs are entirely within the domain normally surveyed by economists. In the context of international trade they have, however, been largely ignored. If taken into account, they modify the conclusions of the doctrine of free trade and justify some protection.

In the European Community the people's preferences are for greater leisure, longer vacations, more generous social security provisions, higher minimum wages, and greater participation in the management of firms by their workers. In so far as these preferences do not interfere with the ability to maintain high rates of growth, free trade can be pursued. But in so far as they are bought at the cost of economic growth and therefore some reduction in income compared with free trade, some closing off, and some management of trade relations, would be legitimate if such closing off can avoid or reduce the losses from and the continuing costs of free trade in a changing world. Private benefits and private costs may diverge from social benefits and social costs; an example of excess social costs would be the relief of the unemployed, the destruction of whole communities, or the harm done to the environment, as a result of a shift in technology.

It could be that the social harmony and homogeneity achieved by maintaining similar values adds to efficiency and makes for higher economic growth. If so, the interventions with trade that lead to the formation of Orwellian trading blocks can, as we shall se in the next section, lead to a *higher* volume of trade between the blocks. The ratio of trade to national income would be reduced, but, as a result of higher incomes, there would be *more* trade.

23. Regional blocs: building or tumbling blocks to globalisation?

I turn now to a discussion of the possible future formation of regional blocs that would manage their external trade and other economic relations. This would, of course, be a retreat from globalisation. The forces that could lead to it are the reactions by Europe and the USA to the dynamic expansion of exports by Japan and the East Asian economies, including China, a slowing down or reversal of economic growth, a revulsion against some of the undesirable manifestations of globalisation, and a reversion to indigenous cultural values. These may take the form of protectionist pressures under the pretext of the need for uniform labour, employment, and environmental standards.

The most recent historical precedent of such bloc formation is that of the inter-war period that followed the pre-1913 period of globalisation. There was the Ottawa Agreement of 1932 and the Sterling Area or, as it was then called, the Sterling Block; there was the French Union; and the USA with the Monroe doctrine. The fragmentation of the world into blocs gave scope to the ruthless rather than the strong. Trade between blocs had been minimized. The exclusion of the Japanese from South and Southeast Asia by the British, French and Dutch was a major cause of Japanese aggression. The exclusion of Germany from the Western blocs contributed to World War 2.

The formation of first the Group of Five and then the Group of Seven and the Summits had not been in the spirit of the multilateral system that had been built in the quarter century after the Second World War. What some observers saw emerging is something that resembles Orwell's picture in *1984*: Oceania, Eurasia and Eastasia. Lester Thurow has pronounced in Davos, which is located in a Swiss valley next to the valley in which Nietzsche pronounced God as dead, that "Gatt is dead," and that multilateralism will be replaced by blocs.

But it is well known that Gatt (or its successor, the World Trade Organization) has nine lives. The creation of the World Trade Organization bears witness to the continued relevance of the multilateral approach. We may echo the British imperial cry, "the king is dead; long live the king!"

At the same time, the liberal world order that the USA had advocated after the war had never been accepted by Europe and Japan. Germany yielded to open her market in return for American troops and defence against the Soviet Union. In the eighties the US herself retreated from liberal trade. The US, Japan, Germany, France and Britain retreated from multilateral institutions. And the recent financial havoc, if repeatet, suggests a widespread retreat from free international capital movements.

If this trend were to continue, we may see the formation of three blocs. Europe with her ex-Colonies in Africa would become "Fortress Europe." The USA, Canada, Mexico, the Caribbean Basin and parts of Central and South America would form a second bloc. Japan and the Pacific Rim, with the four Asian tigers, and possibly ASEAN (Indonesia, Philippines, Malaysia, Singapore, Thailand), and Australia and New Zealand with the Closer Economic Relations Agreement, would form an East Asian-Pacific bloc. (But it must be remembered that Japan's largest market is now the USA, taking 39 per cent of her exports, that South Korea and Taiwan are more integrated with the US than with Japan, and that there are no formal agreements between Japan and any of her neighbours to lower trade barriers.)

At the same time, Japan's trade with the whole of Asia is larger than its trade with North America. Other tentacles of members of these blocs will reach out to outsiders, such as some Caribbean countries to Britain, ex-French colonies to France, the European Union to Central and East Europe, etc. and these will weaken the bloc formation.

There is not much support for such bloc formation at the present time. Singapore and Malaysia, for example, are keen to preserve a multilateral, open trading system and to maintain a strong American presence, and are suspicious of a yen bloc. Japan's attempt at regional bloc formation could be the reaction to fears that there may be a retreat from WTO-led free trade, and that it may be excluded from its two main export markets, the U.S. and Europe.

Much depends on what form these blocs would take; whether, for example, Europe, enlarged by its extension to central and eastern Europe perhaps as far as the Urals, would continue to be, on the whole, an open, outward-looking community, part of a global order, or a highly regulated, bureaucratic bloc; whether the USA, with Canada, Mexico and perhaps South America, would yield to protectionist pressures or resist them. Since a global system cannot be achieved at once, regionalism may point the way to it and be a step towards it. Trade creation would prevail over trade diversion and the competitive power of firms would be strengthened. In this case the regional blocs, instead of being stumbling blocks, would be building blocks for a multilateral system. The introduction of the euro may eventually lead to a shift of dollar reserves into euros and hence to a fall in the value of the dollar vis à vis the euro. This would create problems for North America, Europe and the countries trading with them.

On the other hand, the political interests appeased and created by trade diversion may gather power, oppose trade liberalisation and create inward-looking blocs that manage trade with outsiders. Since trade diversion creates sales and jobs inside the bloc while trade creation destroys them in the short run,[148] the political pressures of particular interests will be for trade diversion, unless the potential export interests are mobilised.

The less likely inward-looking bloc solution need not be as horrifying as Orwell painted it. It can produce a well-working global system. We have succeeded in avoiding major wars for over half a century during at least part of which a considerable amount of trade had been managed, while the global integration before 1913 did not prevent the First World War. The bloc system would permit styles of living to be maintained within each bloc. The Europeans would not have to give up their long holidays, generous social welfare system, workers' participation in management, and minimum wages, or to accept the low rates of return on investment of the Japanese, more interested in long-term presence, and maximizing market shares than in short-term profits. There would be problems of origin, for excluding Japanese producers may mean excluding American products, if they are made by the Japanese in America. The trade between the blocs would be managed through market-sharing and cartel agreements.

A faster rate of growth within each bloc, fostered by homogeneous attitudes, policies and institutions, by greater political

---

[148] This is so because trade creation means that a lower cost supplier outside the bloc replaces a higher cost supplier within the bloc. After a time, which can be quite long, the foreign demand may create different jobs from those eliminated in the high cost country.

stability, and by policies that weaken or defeat special, growth-impeding vested interest groups, though at the expense of some gains from global specialisation, could, as has been argued above, lead to *more* trade between the blocs, even though the ratio of trade to GNP is lower for any given level of income, than in a more open, though more slowly growing, global economy. Regional blocs are also likely to attract more private foreign investment, which would compensate for some of the losses from trade diversion.

But there are drawbacks to such a system. First, its exclusivity, like that in the inter-war period, may encourage aggression. Second, some areas may be left out of all blocs. This is matter of concern, even if it were not to lead to aggression. It is not clear what would be the role of South Asia. India is a potentially important large country in the global economy, but there is no clear role for her in this scenario. What would be the role of Russia and the other ex-Soviet countries? There could be an alignment of Europe with them. And where would China be, in a few decades the largest economy in the world?

There are interesting normative questions arising from the bloc scenario. Apart from the question of the nature of the blocs and their policies, there is the question of the optimum number and optimum size of the blocs. Are three blocs, *ceteris paribus*, better than two? The literature on optimum currency areas is only part of this subject.

Whatever the future fate of regional blocs or of budding region-states such as the European Union, for purposes of analysis and policy we have to look at regions both below and beyond the boundaries of the state. We should analyse events and policies in terms of these regions, both within and beyond countries, rather than only countries or only the globe as a whole. The San Francisco Bay area, Silicon valley, the North Carolina Research Triangle, the Singapore-Johor-Batam-Riau Islands region of Singapore, Malaysia and Indonesia, Hong Kong and Shenzen, the region round Bangalore are significant growth poles. Policies and events cannot be understood unless we look beyond and below national frontiers: Japan's influences in East Asia, India's links with West Asia, relations between countries in the Southern cone of Latin America, beginning with MERCOSUR.

24. The role of conflict

Conflict is normally viewed as destructive of the social order.[149] But it was found that conflict is not necessarily an obstacle to successful development. The pre-Socratic philosopher Heraclitus thought, "war is the father of everything." He wrote: "One must realize that war is common and *conflict is justice* and that all things come to pass in accordance with conflict." (My italics.) Machiavelli entitled a chapter in the *Discourses* "How the Disunion between the Plebs and the Senate Made [the Roman] Republic Free and Powerful." Stuart Hampshire entitled a recent book *Justice is Conflict*.[150] But most authors, including Plato and Aristotle, emphasised order, peace and harmony as the ideal for a social order. More recently, Robert D. Putnam found that the success or failure of regional governments in Italy was "wholly uncorrelated with virtually all measures of political fragmentation, ideological polarization and social conflict." Successful building of social capital through a network of NGOs is not necessarily free of strife.[151]

One may even go further. Conflict, or at least some forms of it, can be regarded as a pillar of democratic societies, as the glue that holds them together. Conflicts can provide society with the "social capital" it needs to be kept together. Albert Hirschman has made a beginning in distinguishing between when conflict is destructive and when constructive. He distinguishes between conflicts about more or less, such as the distribution of income, and conflicts about either/or, such as abortion. Conflict arises inevitably with change. We have seen that globalisation and technical progress benefit some countries, some regions, some sectors, and some groups, and harm others. In free societies, those who suffer will tend to organise themselves and attempt

---

[149] On the role of conflict as a valuable tie, see Albert O. Hirschman (1995) and Paul Streeten (1953). Hirschman's essay also contains a brief history of thought on the subject. The following discussion is indebted to this essay.

[150] Stuart Hampshire (2000).

[151] Robert D. Putnam with Robert Leonardi and Raffaela Y. Nanetti (1992) p. 117.

to regain their position. They will be supported by those who agree with them from a sense of social justice or sympathy. One group is motivated by self-interest, the other by solidarity or a sense of fairness or fellow feelings. The strength of democratic societies derives from this combination and from the conflicts to which it gives rise.

If poverty comprises many more dimensions than lack of income, and includes deprivation of education and health, social exclusion, lack of employment, discrimination against women, environmental degradation (of the soil, water, forests and climate), insecurity, violation of human rights, lack of voice in the counsels of society, and of cultural expression, the chances of conflict over its reduction and eradication are greatly increased. Income can be divided in different proportions and is therefore easier to negotiate and to compromise on than decisions that are subject to an either/or. Ethnic, linguistic, religious and gender divisions and disagreements on voting rights give rise to non-divisible conflicts. Unfortunately, it seems that these types of conflict which are not readily amenable to negotiation and compromise are on the increase.

Though conflict is inevitable and in some forms even desirable, violence and the threat of violence are not desirable. But even the destructive type of conflict that can give rise to violence and revolutions may be inevitable. Anglo-Saxon political and economic theory has been prone to adopt the harmony doctrine, according to which all (legitimate) interests can ultimately be reconciled. Opposed to the Anglo-Saxon conviction of a common good, based on a harmony of interests, is the Continental thought of Marx, Schumpeter and Myrdal who, each on different grounds, reject the concept of "social welfare" or a "common good" as metaphysical nonsense. Their attacks are directed at the various versions of the notion of interest harmony, both as a meaningful concept and as a desirable objective. They not only point out the existence of conflict but often welcome it as a condition of life.

Globalisation reduces the confrontations between capital, management and high skills on the one hand and labour on the other by enabling the former to opt out by going abroad. "The community spirit that is normally needed in a democratic market society tends to be spontaneously generated through the experience of tending the conflicts that are typical of that society," writes Albert Hirschman.[152]

---

[152] Albert Hirschman (1995).

And Dani Rodrik goes on to ask: "But what if globalization reduces the incentives to 'tend' to these conflicts? What if, by reducing the civic engagement of internationally mobile groups, globalization loosens the civic glue that holds societies together and exacerbates social fragmentation? Hence globalization delivers a double blow to social cohesion - first by exacerbating conflict over fundamental beliefs regarding social organization and second by weakening the forces that would normally militate for the resolution of these conflicts through national debate and deliberation."[153] Once again, partial global integration can lead to national disintegration.

Successful adjustment policies call for institutions of managing these conflicts. Adjustment to unfavourable shocks is bound to lead to some losers, who will resist the adjustment measures. Dani Rodrick regards a strategy for institutions of conflict management, together with a high investment strategy, as the most important condition of successful economic performance. [154]

---

[153] Dani Rodrik (1997) p. 70.
[154] Dani Rodrick (1999).

25. Implications for thought and practice

First, there is the need for both transnational, global (or regional) - not just inter-national - institutions and for local ones. I have argued that technology has moved ahead of institutions. Revolutions in transport, travel, communication and information have (partially) unified the world. But institutionally we are stuck with the nation state. The nation state has usurped too many functions, which it can no longer carry out efficiently or humanely. Some of these should be delegated upwards, others downwards. Upward delegation is necessary because technology and private enterprise have become global, while their supervision and regulation have remained national. Global control of the arms trade, a global competition policy, a global investment trust that recycles current account surpluses to capital-starved, developing countries, moves towards a global central bank and towards progressive global taxation, a global energy policy, a global debt facility, a global environmental authority which would bring under one umbrella the numerous environmental bodies, a global investment board that would prevent the lurches from excess capacity to shortages in industries with long gestation periods of investment, commodity price stabilisation, a global technology agency with responsibility to conduct basic research and provide information, a global migration policy, a global health policy that would pledge adequate funds for research and development of vaccines against malaria and other tropical diseases, a global anti-crime and drug policy, are a few examples.

A global anti-monopoly, anti-cartel and anti-restrictive practices policy, for example, would bring international policies in line with national ones. As things are, American companies are prohibited from colluding and forming cartels in the home market but are encouraged by the Webb Pomerane Act to do so against foreign countries. Japanese companies' distribution networks are barriers to trade. Many Japanese firms rely on exclusive local component suppliers. The World Trade Organisation should in principle be able to take on this issue. Now only price discrimination in international trade is ruled out by permitting anti-dumping duties to be imposed. But these are used by most governments as protectionist devices, not to promote competition but to thwart it. Clearly, a competition policy is a task for a supra-national institution, for national governments would be tempted to tailor them to the advantage of their national firms. At the same time, reduced monopoly power will reduce incentives and ability to conduct basic research, increasingly the most important engine of growth in our high-technology age. This may have to be taken over by supra-national agencies or by international research consortia. Research is needed on whether this is necessary and, if so, how it should be done.

Second, the market forces of globalisation should be embedded in democratic institutions and practices that ensure human rights, including those of minorities and women, free expression of the media, facilities for basic education and health care for everyone, and social safety nets.

Third, it is a challenge to design ways of achieving these goals without too many global bureaucrats and to show how to concentrate on processes, procedures, rules, norms and incentives to achieve the objectives.

Fourth, both existing international and future global institutions should be made more participatory, so that the voice of the people is heard. Reform of the UN system in this direction is necessary. One possibility would be the creation of a second chamber in which NGOs would be represented. At the same time, these NGOs themselves should be made fully participatory.

Fifth, where the power distribution in the global arena is very unequal, there should be balancing power centres: for example a Group of Non-Eight to balance the Group of Eight, a Monopolies and Restrictive Practices Commission to balance the power of multinational monopolies and cartels.

Sixth, there is both the obligation and the prudent need (to avoid a backlash to protectionism) to look after the victims of the competitive struggle and of globalisation, and the groups that are hurt by them. This implies two things. First, the speed of progress towards globalisation has to be determined. A slower pace gives more scope to adjustment. Second, where globalisation and liberalisation of trade and finance have caused unemployment, poverty, exclusion and marginalisation, the state should provide various kinds of safety nets, compensation and social insurance, including public works programmes, education and retraining facilities, a programme for changing attitudes and motivation, etc. The answer to the detrimental impact of globalisation is not to stop the process but to take action against its harmful effects, ideally at the global level, but until this is achieved at the national and inter-national level. Since globalisation reduces the public resources available, global taxes should be considered. These measures are necessary in order to avoid not only a backlash to protectionism, but also a deeply and growingly divided society.

Seventh, problems of liberalising international migration in line with the liberalisation of trade and finance should be given a higher priority on the international agenda and examined from the point of view of their impact on the receiving country, as well as that of the migrants themselves and the countries of origin.

Eighth, strategies should aim at the selection of the positive impulses of globalisation and encourage them, while minimizing the impact of the negative impulses, or cushioning the losers against them. This cannot be done by combining globalisation with laissez-faire. The World Trade Organisation's Agreement on Safeguards could be expanded to allow the imposition of temporary trade restrictions to include concerns over labour standards, the environment, and ethical principles. This could be combined with a tightening of the rules on anti-dumping. Or the international agencies dealing with these issues (such as the International Labour Organisation, the United Nations Environment Programme) should be stengthened.

Ninth, for thinkers the task is to explore first, the ways in which different regions, countries, sectors and groups are affected by globalisation, who gains and who loses (absolutely and relatively), and the manner in which ways to protect the weak, the poor and the excluded can be built into the structure of steps towards globalisation from the beginning.

Tenth, they may wish to explore the interaction of the forces for globalisation with the reactions against them, and indicate how the beneficial aspects of globalisation can be combined with preserving the desirable components of local values, traditions and cultural diversity.

Eleventh, the interaction of policies and institutions at five levels should be explored: the micro-micro-level (what goes on inside the firm, the farm, the household), the micro-level, the meso-level (the impact of policies and institutions on different groups and regions) the macro-level and the macro-macro or global level; and the division of duties at each of these levels between private, public (national, international and global), and voluntary agencies. In particular, the impact of globalisation (and of localisation) on the power of the state should be explored.

Twelfth, thought should be given as to how to reduce the heightened insecurity in people's lives that has resulted from a combination of unemployment, precarious job conditions, poverty, inequality, marginalisation and exclusion with sometimes reduced public expenditure on social services: how to match economic globalisation by social globalisation; how to embed globalisation in socially responsive institutions. In addition, there are the great uncertainties created by demographic and environmental threats. A world of six billion people and the dangers of environmental degradation present possibilities of turbulence and upheaval that call for global responses.

Table 1: *Global distribution of wealth: 1960-1994*

	Industrial Countries %	Developing Countries %	FormerUSSR & East. Eur. %
1960	67.3	19.8	12.9
1970	72.2	17.1	10.7
1980	70.7	20.6	8.7
1989	76.3	20.6	3.1
1994	78.7	18.0	3.3

Source: UNDP data base

Table 2: *Global distribution of wealth: 1960-1994: (excluding the former USSR and Eastern Europe)*

	Industrial Countries %	Developing Countries %
1960	77.3	22.7
1970	80.9	19.1
1980	77.4	22.6
1989	78.8	21.2
1994	81.4	18.6

Source: UNDP data base

Table 3: *Growth rate of GDP per head, as compared with the 1960-71 average*

	1972-81	1982-91
All countries (57)		
Decade ratio higher	18	10
Decade ratio lower	39	47
All non-oil exporting countries (48)		
Decade ratio higher	11	7
Decade ratio lower	37	41
OECD countries (20)		
Decade ratio higher	1	2
Decade ratio lower	19	18
Latin America (10)		
Decade ratio higher	4	1
Decade ratio lower	6	9
East and South East Asia (7)		
Decade ratio higher	5	3
Decade ratio lower	2	4

Source: John Eatwell "International Capital Liberalisation: an Evaluation" A Report to UNDP (SSA no. 96-049, April 1996; David Felix "financial globalisation versus free trade: the case for the Tobin tax," UNCTAD discussion paper, no. 108; using data source World Bank, *World Tables.*

26. Definitions of globalisation

The most succinct definition of globalisation is due to Manuel Castells: "The power to act instantaneously at a distance."

He also provides a fuller definition: the process by which in a given dimension of society, for instance the economy, its core activities acquire the technological and organization potential to work as a unit in real time on a planetary scale. Manuel Castells "European Cities, the Informational Society, and the Global Economy" *New Left Review* March-April 1994.

(Economic) integration is synonymous with (economic) globalisation, "the tendency for the economic significance of political boundaries to diminish." (David Henderson, mimeographed).

"The growing interpenetration of markets." (Manuel R. Agosin and Diana Tussie.)

"It is true that the immense cheapening of international transport and communication - the ability to communicate instantaneously by voice, by fax-transmitted paper or by electronic bits at very low costs - together with the lowering of tariffs and the (very partial) dismantling of trade barriers under the aegis of the GATT, has been one crucial factor intensifying competitive pressures on manufacturers and bankers alike, and it is a factor aptly named 'globalization.'" (Ronald Dore)

"The increasing internationalisation of the production, distribution and marketing of goods and services." (R. G. Harris, Globalization, Trade and Income, *Canadian Journal of Economics*, November 1993.)

"When it comes to acid rain or oil spills or depleted fisheries or tainted groundwater or fluorocarbon propellants or radiation leaks or toxic wastes or sexually transmitted diseases, national frontiers are simply irrelevant." (Benjamin Barber *Jihad vs. McWorld*, p. 12.)

"'Globalisation' is the growth, or more precisely the accelerated growth, of economic activity across national and regional political boundaries. It finds expression in the increased movement of tangible and intangible goods and services, including ownership rights, via trade and investment, and often of people, via migration." (Charles Oman, "The Policy Challenges of Globalisation and Regionalisation.")

"Globalization is, briefly, the intensification of economic, political, social, and cultural relations across borders." (Hans-Henrik Holm and George Sørensen, "Whose World Order?")

"Techno-globalism" defined to encompass the growing degree to which "multinational firms are exploiting their technology globally and, to a lesser though increasing degree, are gaining access to new technology globally through the world-wide diffusion of R&D and through collaboration." (Sylvia Ostry and Richard R. Nelson, *Techno-nationalism and Techno-Globalism: Conflict and Cooperation.*)

Globalisation as increased internationalisation of economic intercourse vs. globalisation in the broad sense includes "every aspect of social activity - be it communication, ecological maters, commerce, regulation, ideology or whatever." (Jan Aart Scholte, quoted in Holt and Sørensen.)

"Globalization...is driven by a widespread push toward the liberalization of trade and capital markets, increasing internationalization of corporate production and distribution strategies, and technological change that is rapidly dismantling barriers to the international tradability of goods and services and the mobility of capital." (Zia Qureshi, *Finance and Development*, March 1996.)

"The manifestations of globalisation include the spatial reorganisation of production, the interpenetration of industries across borders, the spread of financial markets, the diffusion of identical consumer goods to distant countries, massive transfers of population within the South as well as from the South and the East to the West, resultant conflicts between immigrant and established communities in formerly tight-knit neigbourhoods, and an emerging worldwide preference for democracy." (James H Mittelman, *Third World Quarterly*, September 1994.)

"Globalization is the process whereby the world's people are becoming increasingly interconnected in all facets of their lives - cultural, economic, political, technological, and environmental." (George C. Lodge, "Managing Globalization in the Age of Interdependence.")

"In common parlance, globalisation is often equated with growing integration, of national economies. But as employed here, the concept also refers to the rapid spread world wide of some dominant social, cultural and political norms and practices." (*Social Movements in Development*, ed by Staffan Lindberg and Arni Sverrison.)

"Globalisation...refers to a set of emerging conditions in which value and wealth are increasingly being produced and distributed within world-wide corporate networks." "Globalisation refers to the stage now reached and the forms taken today by what is known as 'international production," namely value-adding activities owned or controlled and organised by a firm (or group of firms) outside its (or their) national boundaries." (TEP The Technology/Economy Programme, Technology and The Economy; The Key Relationships, OECD Paris 1992.)

"According to the various points of view, we could globalization to mean the establishment of a global market for goods and capital, the universal character of competing technologies, the progression towards a global system of production, the political weight that the global system carries in the competition for global or regional hegemonies, the cultural aspect of universalization, etc....In its broadest sense globalization refers to the existence of relations between the different regions of the world and, as a corollary, the reciprocal influence that societies exert upon one another." (Samir Amin, "The Challenge of Globalization," *Review of International Political Economy*, Routledge, Summer 1996.)

"[G]lobalization identifies both a process in which the production and financial structures of countries are becoming interlinked by an increasing number of cross-border transactions to create an international division of labour in which national wealth creation comes, increasingly, to depend on economic agents in other countries, and the ultimate stage of economic integration where such dependence has reached its spatial limit." (Paul Bairoch and Richard Kozul-Wright, "Globalization Myths: Some Historical Reflections on Integration, Industrialization   and   Growth   in   the   World   Economy." UNCTAD/OSG/DP/113. March 1996.)

"The term 'globalization' which became *au courant* during the 1980s, while never precisely defined, is meant to convey the increasing linkages among countries or the deeper integration of the world economy by trade, finance, direct investment and technology. Interdependence also involves an increasing interrelationship among major influences of the world economic system, with monetary policy affecting trade policy, feeding back into monetary and fiscal policy." (Sylvia Ostry, "Technological Change and International Economic Institutions," Discussion Paper Number 2, December 1995, Centre for International Studies, University of Toronto.)

"Globalization ...is a complex process resulting from the rapidly increasing flow of goods, money, people, ideas and images across national boundaries...globalization is creating a patchwork of connected and overlapping but nevertheless distinct worlds...The one thing they have in common is that, thanks to modern communication and transportation technologies, they pay little heed to geography and conventional political boundaries." (Michael Clough, *Shaping American Foreign Relations: The Critical Role of the Southeast*, Stanley Foundation, *New American Dialogue*, Muscatine, Iowa, 1996.)

"Globalization as a term refers to the growinginteraction of countries in world trade, foreign direct investment and capital markets. The globalization process has been abetted by technological advances in transport and communications, and by a rapid liberalization and deregulation of trade and capital flows, both at the national and international levels." (Introduction to "Globalization and Liberalization: Effects of International Economic Relations on Poverty. UNDCTAF/ECDC/ PA/4/Rev 1/ Geneva 1996.)

"'Globalization' is a myth suitable for a world without illusions, but it is also one that robs us of hope." (Paul Hirst and Grahame Thompson,

Globalization in Question: The International Economy and the Possibilities of Governance Cambridge: Polity Press, 1996.)

"Globalisation is...defined as the process by which enterprises (related or unrelated) become interdependent and interlinked globally through strategic alliances and international networks...[D]eregulation and privatisation are seen as promoting international trade and investment, or internationalisation - or, in the language of some, 'globalisation.'" (Helen O'Neill, "Globalisation, Competitiveness and Human Security: Challenges for Development Policy and InstitutionalChange" in *Globalisation, Competitiveness and Human Security*, edited by Cristóbal Kay, London-Portland OR: Frank Cass, 1997, pp. 20, 21.)

Globalisation is defined as "that loose combination of free trade agreements, the Internet and the integration of financial markets that is erasing borders and uniting the world into a single, lucrative, but brutally competitive marketplace." Thomas Friedman, "Revolt of the Wannabes: Globalisation Suffers a Backlash," *The New York Times*, 7 February 1996.)

"Globalisation and technological change are spawning new sources of competition, deregulation is changing the rules of competition in many industries, markets `are becoming more complex and unpredictable and information flows in a tightly wired world permit companies to sense and react to competitors at a faster rate." (George Day and David Reibstein, "Keeping Ahgead in the Competitive Game," *Financial Times*, Mastering Management No. 18, 1995-96, p. 2.)

"Globalisation is the forging of a multiplicity of linkages and interconnections between the states and societies which make up themodern world system. The process by which events, decisions and activities in one part of the world can come to have significant consequences for individuals and communities in quite distant parts of the globe." (A. McGrew, "The Third World in the New Global Order," in T. Allen and A. Thomas (eds.) *Poverty and Development in the 1990s*, Oxford: Oxford University Press in association with the Open University, 1992, p. 262.)

Globalisation is defined as "the entirety of such universal processes as technological transformation, interdependence caused by mass communications, trade and capital flows, homogenisation and standardisation of production and consumption, the predominance of the world market in trade, investment and other corporate transactions, spatial and institutional integration of markets, and growing identity or similarity of economic regulations, institutions and policies. (Mihaly Simai, "Globalisation, Multilateral Cooperation and the Development Process: The UN Agenda and End-of-Century Realities," *Working Paper No. 63*, Institute for World Economics, Hungarian Academy of Sciences, April 1996, p.7)

"Basically, globalization indicates a qualitative deepening of the internationalization process, strengthening the functional and weakening the territorial dimension of development." (Björn Hettne Report of the UNRISD International Conference on "Globalization and Citizenship" UNRISD, Geneva, September 1997.)

"Globalization can be defined as a structural shift in the spatial organization of socio-economic and political activity towards transcontinental or inter-regional patterns of relations, interaction and the exercise of power." (Anthony McGrew, "Globalization: Conceptualizing a Moving Target" Paper prepared for a Seminar on International Solidarity an Globalization: In Search of New Strategies," Stockholm, October 1997, mimeo, p. 14.)

UNRISD lists six key trends of globalisation: the spread of liberal democracy; the dominance of market forces; the integration of the global economy; the transformation of production systems and labour markets; the speed of technological change; and the media revolution and consumerism. (United Nations Research Institute for Social Development *States of Disarray: The Social Effects of Globalisation*, Geneva, United Nations, 1995.)

"There is agreement that 'globalization' refers to the consequences of two phenomena that, in combination, have resulted in the global 'compression of time and space.' The first is technological changes in the processing and dissemination of information related to finance and production. The second is the international spread of the technical competence necessary to use these advances efficiently." Jay R. Mandle and Louis Ferleger, "Preface" *The Annals of the American*

Academy of Political and Social Science, volume 570 Thousand Oaks, London, New Delhi: Sage Publications July 2000 p. 8.

"Globalization is the twofold process of the particularization of the universal and the universalization of the particular." Roland Robertson *Globalization: Social Theory and Global Culture* Sage pp. 177-178.

"Globalization is an untotalizable totality which intensifies binary relations between its parts – mostly nations, but also regions and groups, which, however, continue to articulate themselves on the model of 'national entities' (rather thn in terms of social classes for example))." Fredric Jameson Preface in *The Culture of Globalization* ed. Fredric Jameson and Masao Miyoshi. Durham, N.C.: Duke University Press p. xii.

"Globalization is the geographic dispersion of industrial and service activities (for example, research and development, sourcing of inputs, production and distribution) and the cross-border networking of companies (for example, through joint ventures and the sharing of assets)." Graham Bannock, R. E. Baxter, and Evan Davis *Dictionary of Economics*. New York: Wiley 1998.

Daniel Yergin, author of *The Commanding Heights*, wrote in the May 18, 1998 issue of *Newsweek*, "We are now beginning a reality beyond globalization – the world of globality." He wanted to move on from the description of a process, globalization, to a state of being. Globality suggests a condition of community and interconnections. The 1999 theme at the World Economic Forum in Davos was "Responsible Globality." Globality is not yet in the dictionaries.

References

Annable James (1996) "No Need to Fear Lower Unemployment" *The Wall Street Journal*, 21 August.

Atkinson Anthony B. (1999) "Is Rising Inequality Inevitable? A Critique of the Transatlantic Consensus" *WIDER Annual Lectures 3* UNU WIDER.

Axelrod R. (1984) *The Evolution of Cooperation Basic Books*, New York.

Bairoch Paul (1993) "International Industrialization Levels from 1750 to 1980" *Journal of European Economic History*, Brighton Wheatsheaf.

Bairoch Paul and Richard Kozul-Wright (undated) Globalization Myths: Some Historical Reflection on Integration, Industrialization and Growth in the World Economy, UNCTAD/OSG/DP, 113.

Barber Benjamin (1995) *Jihad vs. McWorld*, Times Books, Random House, New York.

Blaug Mark (1998) review of *Equilibrium and Economic Theory* edited by Giovanni Caravale, *The Economic Journal*, vol. 108 No 451 November 1998.

CEPA News (1997), The Newsletter of the Center for Economic Policy Analysis, vol. 1 No. 1 Spring p. 2.

Bourgignon François and Christian Morrison (1989) *External Trade and Income Distribution* Paris OECD.

Card David and Alan B. Krueger (1995) *Myth and Measurement: The New Economics of the Minimum Wage* Princeton: Princeton University Press April.

Cassidy John (1999) "Wall Street Follies" *The New Yorker* September 13.

Center for Economic Policy Analysis at the New School for Social Research *CEPA News (1997)*, The Newsletter of the Center for Economic Policy Analysis, vol. 1 No. 1 Spring 1997.

Chuta Enyinna and Carl Liedholm (1985) *Employment and Growth in Small-Scale Industry* Macmillan, London.

Cooper Richard N. (1985) "Panel discussion: the prospects for international policy coordination," *International Economic Policy Coordination* edited by William H. Buiter and Richard C. Marston, Cambridge University Press, Cambridge, England.

Crossette Barbara (1997) "The Unreal Thing. Un-American Ugly Americans" *The New York Times Week in Review* May 11th

De Soto Hernando (1989) *The Other Path; The Invisible Revolution in the Third World;* Harper & Row, New York, I. B. Tauris, London.

Dore Ronald (1996) Comments on Lord Dahrendorf's lecture, mimeographed.

East Africa Economic Review (1989) Special Issue on Contract Farming and Smallholder Outgrower Schemes in Eastern and Southern Africa of the, Economics Department, University of Nairobi, August.

Eatwell John (1995) "The International Origins of Unemployment," in J. Michie and J.G. Smith, editors, *Managing the Global Economy*, Oxford University Press.

The Economist (1996) "Trade and Wages," December 7th.

The Economist (1997) November 1st.

Falk Richard (1996) "Revisioning Cosmopolitanism" in Martha Nussbaum and others *For Love of Country: Debating the Limits of Patriotism* edited by Joshua Cohen Beacon Press Boston.

Farrell M. J.(1987) "Information and the Coase Theorem," *Journal of Economic Perspectives*, 1, Number 2 Fall pp. 113-129.

Feenstra Robert C. (1998) "Integration of Trade and Disintegration of Production in the Global Economy," *The Journal of Economic Perspectives*, volume 12 Number 4, Fall 1998.

Friedlander Daniel, David H. Greenberg and Philip K. Robins (1997) "Evaluating Government Training Programs for the Economically Disadvantaged" *Journal of Economic Literature* December, Volume xxxv Number 4.

Friedman Thomas L. (1997) "Roll Over Hawks and Doves" *The New York Times* February 2.

Geertz Clifford (1969) "Myrdal's Mythology" *Encounter* July.

Garrett Geoffrey and Peter Lange (1995) "Internationalization, institutions, and political change," *International Organization,* 49, Autumn.

Garrett Geoffrey (1995) "Capital mobility, trade, and the domestic politics of economic policy," *International Organization,* 49,4, Autumn.

Giddens Anthony (1995) "Affluence, Poverty and the Idea of a Post-Scarcity Society," United Nations Research Institute for Social Development, Discussion Paper DP 63, May.

Glover David J. (1984) "Contract Farming and Smallholder Outgrower Schemes in Less Developed Countries" *World Development* volume 12 Numbers 11/12, November/December.

Glover David J. (1987) "Increasing the Benefits to Smallholders from Contract Farming: Problems for Farmers' Organizations and Policy Makers," *World Development*, Vol. 15 No. 4.

Goldsmith Arthur (1985) "The Private Sector and Rural Development: Can Agribusiness Help the Small Farmer?" *World Development*, volume 13 Numbers 10/11 October/November.

Haq Mahbub ul, Inge Kaul and Isabelle Grunberg (editors) (1996) *The Tobin Tax: Coping with Financial Volatility*, Oxford University Press.

Hampshire Stuart (2000) *Justice is Conflict* Princeton: Princeton University Press.

Health and Development (1989) "An Interview with Hernando de Soto" volume 1 Number 1 March/April.

Henderson David (1993) "International Migration: Appraising Current Policies" Draft 4 November.

Herbert Bob (1995) "A Nation of Nitwits," *New York Times*, March 1 p. A 19.

Hicks J. R. (1935) "The Theory of Monopoly" Econometrica.

Hirschman Albert O. (1995) "Social Conflicts as Pillars of Democratic Market Societies" in *A Propensity to Self-Subversion*, Harvard University Press, Cambridge Massachusetts and London, England.

Hopkins Michael (1989) "Comments on Professor S. Kannappan" *in Fighting Urban Unemployment in Developing Countries*, edited by Bernard Salome, Development Centre of the OECD, Paris.

IMF Survey, (1994) Nov 14.

Inter-American Development Bank (IDB) (1996), Economic and Social Progress in Latin America – 1996 Report Washington DC November.

International Labour Office (1972) *Employment, Incomes and Equality: A Strategy for Increasing Productive Employment in Kenya*, Geneva: International Labour Office.

Kanbur Ravi (2001) "Economic Policy, Distribution and Poverty: The Nature of Disagreement" forthcoming in *World Development*.

Kashyap S.P (1988) "Growth of Small-size Enterprises in India: Its Nature and Content" *World Development*, vol. 16, No. 6, June.

Keynes J. M. (1929) *The Economics of our Grandchildren.*

Keynes J. M. (1933) "National Self-Sufficiency," Yale Review, Summer, and *New Statesman and Nation*, 8th and 15th July 1933. *Collected Writings of John Maynard Keynes*, Volume XXI, [1933] Activities 1931-39, edited by Donald Moggeridge. London: Macmillan and Cambridge University Press 1982, p. 237.

Lipton Michael (1985) "The Prisoners' Dilemma and Coase's Theorem: A Case for Democracy in Less Developed Countries?" in *Economy and Democracy*, edited by R.C.O. Matthews, St. Martin's Press, New York.

Khan A. R. (1996) "Globalization and Urban Employment: Some Issues in an Asian Perspective," Paper for the UNDP/Habitat Round Table in Marmaris, Turkey, 19-21 April.

Lall Sanjaya (1985) "A Study of Multinational and Local Firm Linkages in India" *Multinationals, Technology and Exports* Macmillan, London.

Landell-Mills Pierre and Ismail Serageldin (1992) "Governance and the External Factor" *Proceedings of the World Bank Annual Conference on Development Economics 1991 Supplement to the World Bank Economic Review and the World Bank Research Observer*, the World Bank, Washington D.C.

Lateef K. Sawar (1991) "Comment on 'Governance and Development,' by Boetninger" *Proceedings of the World Bank Annual Conference on Development Economics 1991, Supplement to the World Bank Economic Review and Research Observer*, The World Bank, Washington D.C.

Liedholm Carl and Donald Mead (1987) *Small Scale Industries in Developing Countries: Empirical Evidence and Policy Implications* International Development Paper No. 9, Department of Agricultural Economics, Michigan State University, East Lansing, Michigan, 48824.

Lohr Steve (1999) "Computer Age Gains Respect of Economists" *The New York Times* front page April 14.

López-Mejía Alejandro (1999) *Large Capital Flows: A Survey of the Causes, Consequences and Public Responses*, IMF Working Paper 99/17.

Maddison Angus (1989) *The World Economy in the Twentieth Century* Paris: OECD Development Centre.

Maddison Angus (1995) *Monitoring the World Economy*, Paris: OECD Publications.

Madrick Jeff (1998) "Computers: Waiting for the Revolution" *The New York Review of Books* March 26.

Maizels A (1963) *Industrial Growth and World Trade*, Cambridge: Cambridge University Press.

Messner Dirk and Franz Nuscheler (1996) *Global Governance*, Development and Peace Foundation, Policy Paper 2, Bonn, Germany.

Minogue Kenneth (2000) "A modern passion?" *Times Literary Supplement* October 13.

Nayyar Deepak (1995) *Globalisation: The Past in Our Present*, Presidential Address to the Seventy-Eighth Annual Conference of the Indian Economic Association, Chandigarh 28-30 December.

Nelson Joan (1991) *Proceedings of the World Bank Annual Conference on Development Economics 1991 Supplement to the World Bank Economic Review and the World Bank Research Observer*, the World Bank, Washington D.C.

The New York Times (1989) 9 November 1989.

The New York Times (1996) 10 December "With Major Math Proof, Brute Computers Show Flash of Reasoning Power" by Gina Kolata, Section C1.

The New York Times (1999) September 5 1999.

The New Yorker (1995) Feb. 6.

Ohlin Göran (1994) "A Plea for Realism in Discussing International Cooperation," Participant Paper 52 for the Roundtable on Global Change, Saltsjöbaden, UNDP 22-24 July.

Oman Charles (undated) "The Policy Challenges of Globalisation and Regionalisation" OECD Development Centre, Policy Brief No. 11.

O'Rourke Kevin, Alan Taylor and Jeffrey Williamson (1996), "Factor Price Convergence in the Late Nineteenth Century," *International Economic Review*.

Orwell George (1946) "Politics and the English Language," *Collected Essays*, Mercury Books London 1961,

Ostry Sylvia (1995) "Technological Change and International Economic Institutions," Discussion Paper No. 2, December, Centre for International Studies, Toronto.

Peattie Lisa (1987) "An Idea in Good Currency and How it Grew: The Informal Sector" *World Development*, volume 15 Number 7, July.

Polanyi Karl (1944) *The Great Transformation*, Boston, MA Beacon Press.

Riding Alan (1988) "Peruvians Combating Red Tape' *The New York Times*, July 24.

Putnam Robert D. with Robert Leonardi and Raffaela Y. Nanetti (1993) *Making Democracy Work,* Princeton, New Jersey: Princeton University Press.

Rao Mohan (1995) "Globalization: a View from the South" mimeo, December.

Report of the Commission on Global Governance (1995) *Our Global Neighbourhood*, Oxford: Oxford University Press.

Report of the Commission on Global Governance *Update (1994)* September.

Robbins Donald (1996) "Evidence on Trade and Wages in the Developing World," OECD Development Centre Technical Paper No. 119. December.

Rodrick Dani (1995) "Getting interventions right: how South Korea and Taiwan grow rich." *Growth Policy* No. 20 April.

Rodrik Dani (1996) "Why Do More Open Economies Have Bigger Governments?" NBER Working Paper No. 5537, Cambridge, Massachusetts, Revised March.

Rodrik Dani (1997), *Has Globalization Gone Too Far?* Institute for International Economics, Washington, D.C.: March.

Rodrick Dani (1999) *The New Global Economy and Developing Countries: Making Openness Work* Washington D.C.: The Overseas Development Council.

Rodrik Dani (2000) "How Far Will International Economic Integration Go?" *Journal of Economic Perspectives* volume 14 Number 1 winter.

Ruggie John G. (1995) "At Home Abroad, Abroad at Home: International Liberalization and Domestic Stability in the New World Economy" *Millenium: Journal of International Studies*, 24, no. 3.

Sabel Charles F. (1987) "Changing Models of Economic Efficiency and their Implications for Industrialization in the Third World," Department of City and Regional Planning, MIT, Cambridge, and in *Development, Democracy, and the Art of Trespassing: Essays in Honor of Albert O. Hirschman*, edited by Alejandro Foxley, Michael S. McPherson, and Guillermo O'Donnell, University of Notre Dame Press, Notre Dame, Indiana, 1986,

Schoeni Robert, Kevin McCarthy and George Vernez (undated) "The Mixed Economic Progress of Immigrants," the Rand Corporation's Center for Research on Immigration Policy.

Sichel Daniel (1997) *The Computer Revolution*, quoted in *The Economist* September 13 1997.

Simon Julian L. (1989) *The Economic Consequences of Immigration*, Basil Blackwell.

Sinha Radha Peter Pearson, Gopal Kadekodi and Mary Gregory (1979) *Income Distribution, Growth and Basic Needs in India*, Croom Helm, London.

Solow Robert M. (1990) *The Labor Market as a Social Institution*, Basil Blackwell, Cambridge, Massachusetts.

Stalker Peter (1994) *The Work of Strangers*, ILO Geneva.

Statistical Abstract of the United States (1999) Washington, D.C., US Government Printing Office.

Stiglitz Joseph (1998) "Bad Private-Sector Decisions" *Wall Street Journal*, February 4.

Stiglitz Joseph (1998) "More Instruments and Broader Goals: Moving Toward the Post-Washington Consensus" The 1998 WIDER Annual Lecture. Helsinki, Finland, January 7 mimeo.

Strassman Paul (1997) *The Squandered Computer* as reported in *The Economist*, September 13 1997.

Streeten Paul (1953) Appendix to Gunnar Myrdal *The Political Element in the Development of Economic Theory* Routledge & Kegan Paul, London.

Streeten Paul (1989 a) "International Cooperation," in *Handbook of Development Economics*, volume 2, editors: Hollis Chenery and T. N. Srinivasan, North Holland, Amsterdam.

Paul Streeten (1989 b) "The Judy Trick," in *Markets, Morals and Public Policy* editors Lionel Orchard and Robert Dare, Annandale, NSW: the Federation Press.

Streeten Paul (1993) "Markets and States: Against Minimalism" *World Development*, Vol. 21, No. 8, August.

Streeten Paul (1995), *Thinking About Development*, Cambridge University Press, Cambridge, Second Lecture.

Streeten Paul (1997) "Nongovernmental Organizations and Development" *The Annals of the American Academy of Political and Social Science The Role of NGOs: Charity and Empowerment* special Editors: Jude L. Fernando and Alan W. Heston, November 1997, Volume 554.

TEP (1992), The Technology/Economy Programme *Technology and the Economy; The Key Relationships* Paris: OECD.

Tendler Judith (1987) "The remarkable convergence of fashion on small enterprise and the informal sector: what are the implications for policy?" mimeo.

Tharoor Shashi (1997) *India: From Midnight to the Millennium* Arcade Publishing.

Uchitelle Louis (1996) "What Has the Computer Done for Us Lately?" *The New York Times Week in Review* Sunday December 4 section 4.

United Nations Development Programme (1995) *Human Development Report.*

United Nations Development Programme (2000) *Human Development Report.*

UNRISD (1995) *States of Disarray; The social effects of globalization* Geneva.

Vidal Gore (1992) *Screening History*, Cambridge, Mass. Harvard University Press.

Wade Robert (1996) "Globalization and its Limits: Reports of the Death of the National Economy Are Greatly Exaggerated," in *National Diversity and Global Capitalism*, edited by Suzanne Berger and Ronald Dore, Cornell University Press, Ithaca and London.

Wade Robert (1999) "National Power, Coercive Liberalism and 'Global Finance'" *International Politics: Current Issues and Enduring Themes*, edited by Robert Art and Robert Jervis, Addison Wesley Kaufman.

Williamson Jeffrey (1995) "The Evolution of Global Labour Markets since 1830: Background Evidence and Hypotheses." *Explorations in Economic History.*

Williamson Jeffrey (1996) "Globalisation, Convergence and History," *Journal of Economic History.*

Williamson Jeffrey G. (1997) "Globalization and Inequality: Past and Present," *The World Bank Research Observer*, volume 12 Number 2 August.

Wood Adrian (1994) *North-South Trade, Employment and Inequality: Changing Fortunes in a Skill-Driven World.* Oxford: Clarendon Press.

Wood Adrian (1995) "How Trade Hurt Unskilled Workers" *The Journal of Economic Perspectives*, volume 9 No.3, Nashville TN, Summer.

Wood Adrian (1998) "Globalisation and the Rise in Labour Market Inequalities" *The Economic Journal*, vol. 108 No. 450, September.

Woodall Pam (1996) "A Survey of the World Economy: The hitchhiker's guide to cybernomics" *The Economist* September 28.

World Bank (1989) *Sub-Saharan Africa: From Crisis to Sustainable Growth. A Long-Term Perspective Study*, Washington, D.C.

World Bank *World Development Report* (1993) Washington D.C.

World Bank *World Development Report* (1995) Washington D.C.

World Investment Report (1996) United Nations Conference on Trade and Development, Geneva.

Yunus Muhammad (1999) Banker to the Poor. Micro-Lending and the Battle Against World Poverty New York: Public Affairs with Alan Jolis.

Zakaria Fareed (2000) "Globalization Grows Up and Gets Political" *The New York Times* Op-Ed December 31, Section 4.

Index of Names

Index of Subjects